Osprey Modelling • 5

Modelling the Matilda Infantry Tank

Mark Bannerman

Consultant editor Robert Oehler • Series editors Marcus Cowper and Nikolai Bogdanovic

First published in Great Britain in 2004 by Osprey Publishing,
Midland House, West Way, Botley, Oxford OX2 0PH, UK
44-02 23rd St, Suite 219, Long Island City, NY 11101, USA
Email: info@ospreypublishing.com

Transferred to digital print on demand 2010

First published 2004
1st impression 2004

Printed and bound by Cadmus Communications, USA

A CIP catalogue record for this book is available from the British Library

ISBN: 978 1 84176 758 1

Editorial by Ilios Publishing, Oxford, UK (www.iliospublishing.com)
Design by Servis Filmsetting Ltd, Manchester, UK
Proofreading by Richard Windrow
Index by Alison Worthington
Originated by Global Graphics, Prague, Czech Republic

Photographic credits
The following credit abbreviations refer to the photographs that appear in this work:

AS	Arthur Sekula
BR	Bill Renfrew
CS	Chris Shillito (Armour in Focus)
CM	Charles Moors
DC	David Crisp
EP	Éric Peytavin
HM	Harold McIntyre
JH	John Howells
JM	Juan Luis Mercadal Pons
JWB	Jan-Willem De Boer
LM	Lionel Marco
MC	Mark Cooper
MG	Michael Grieve
MB	Mark Bannerman
PZ	Patrick Zimmerling (www.jagdtiger.de)
RB	Rick Bennett
SD	Sean Dunnage
SG	Saul Garcia
SZ	Steve Zaloga
UA	Ulf Andersson

Acknowledgements
I would like to thank the following people for their tremendous assistance in helping me put the 'Tilly' project together. In Canada: Arthur Sekula;
Mark (Ausf. IV) Cooper; Ron Volstad; Sean Dunnage; Paul 'bookman' Fraser; Chris Johnson; Kevin McLaughlin (Ultracast); Éric Peytavin;
David E. Brown; Mark Bourque (Ausf. III), Cranky John and and Chatty Mike at Maritime Hobbies; Mark Stares (Ausf II); Charles Moors;
Jeff at Econo-colour; and Gerald Mann. In the UK: Chris Shillito (Armour in Focus); Robert Lockie; Gordon Brown (Cromwell Models);
Derek Hanson (Accurate Armour); David Fletcher. In the USA: Steve Zaloga, Rick Bennet. In Japan, Hideki Yoshida. In Europe: Juan Luis
Mercadal Pons; Lionel Marco; Saul Garcia; Patrick Zimmerling; Jan-Willem De Boer. In Australia: Michael Grieve, Ian Stuart; John Howells;
David Crisps; Paul Handel; Bill Renfrew; and Peter Brown. Plus, the missing-lynx.com members and the Maritime Modelers crew – thanks for
the help, gents! Last but not least, thanks to my lovely, patient wife Elizabeth, my folks Pat and Bill, and my brother Paul (hup hup!)

FRONT COVER Matilda 'Frog' montage, by Ulf Andersson.

FOR A CATALOGUE OF ALL BOOKS PUBLISHED BY
OSPREY MILITARY AND AVIATION PLEASE CONTACT:

Osprey Direct, c/o Random House Distribution Center,
400 Hahn Road, Westminster, MD 21157
Email: uscustomerservice@ospreypublishing.com

Osprey Direct, The Book Service Ltd, Distribution Centre,
Colchester Road, Frating Green, Colchester, Essex, CO7 7DW
Email: customerservice@ospreypublishing.com

www.ospreypublishing.com

Contents

Introduction

Although models of the Infantry Tank Mk. II (A12), better known as the Matilda, have been around for more than 30 years, it is only recently that manufacturers have recognized the scale modeller's interest in this tank. In response to this, a wide range of aftermarket products and kits have appeared. The growing appeal of the Matilda tank to scale modellers is also a reflection of its contribution to early British tank development, and it remains one of the most important and interesting infantry tanks of World War II.

Although the Matilda is predominantly remembered for its vital role in the Western Desert campaign – hence the nickname 'Queen of the Desert' – it also saw action in the opening days of the war in Northern France, in the Pacific and on the Eastern Front. Matilda variants appeared in many forms, including mine-clearing, demolition, flame-throwing, trench-crossing and gap-bridging. Matildas were used in combat by the British, Russians, Australians, and even the Germans, who pressed small numbers of captured examples into service. The Matilda is a relatively well-documented and photographed infantry tank, and its versatility offers the modeller a wide range of construction and conversion alternatives, painting possibilities and a slew of vignette and diorama options.

In this book, several different Matilda kit offerings will be presented, and the construction, detailing, painting and finishing processes will be described for each. Hints and tips on making a model look more realistic, personalising a model with accessories and figures, and ways to create an appropriate base and setting will also be covered.

View of the upper rear hull of Bovington Tank Museum's fully restored Matilda A I I, at TankFest 2000. Note the BEF G3/G4 two-green colour scheme. (CS)

ABOVE A fully restored Matilda A12 ('Golden Miller') belonging to Bovington Tank Museum in operation at TankFest 2000. (JWB)

BELOW The Bovington Matilda A11 at TankFest 2000. (JWB)

A Matilda on display at the Victory Memorial in Moscow. (PZ)

A brief history of the Matilda

In 1935, Vickers-Armstrong Ltd. was commissioned to design a well-armoured tank armed with one machine gun. The outcome was the Infantry Tank Mk. I (A11). Almost 140 of the A11s were built. However, its slow speed, lack of anti-tank capabilities, mechanical drawbacks and ineffective performance led to the development of a larger, well-armed and well-armoured infantry tank. The result was a heavier, improved tank, the Infantry Tank Mk. II Matilda A12 – or Matilda II. The Matilda II had a crew of four (commander, gunner, loader and driver), weighed 59,000 lbs, was armed with a 2-pdr gun and a 7.92mm Besa machine gun, and had a maximum speed of 15 mph. Almost 3,000 Matildas IIs were built, and the tank passed through five marks. Variants of the Matilda II include the Baron, Scorpion, Canal Defence Light (CDL), bulldozer, the Hedgehog, and the flamethrower Frog (see also the table on page 67).

Matilda nomenclature

Nomenclature is a frequent point of confusion, as three styles of name were generally used for the Matilda. Originally known as the A11 and A12, the term Matilda sees to have been commonly used from early on. The first official adoption of 'Matilda' was on 11 June 1940 and set out the following new designations:

Infantry Tank Mk.I   previously known as A11 or Matilda I
Infantry Tank Mk.II   previously known as A12 or Matilda II
Infantry Tank Mk.IIA previously known as A12 or Matilda II

The next name change came in July 1941, and used names for each type of tank, with 'marks' denoting the changes made. The style names and changes can be summarised as:

Original	June 1940	July 1941	Details of changes
A12	Infantry II	Matilda I	AEC engine, co-axial Vickers
A12	Infantry IIA	Matilda II	AEC engine, co-axial BESA, turret vent fan
A12	Infantry IIA	Matilda III	Leyland engine
		Matilda IV	Rigid engine mounting, turret lamp deleted
		Matilda V	Westinghouse air servo for gear change system

Production records are often confusing due to the change of engines. Some Matilda IV vehicles may have been Matilda IIIs: the records are unclear. Also, the Matilda V is not listed as being built, so may have been converted.

Peter Brown

Tools and materials

Essential tools

Although there are many expensive (and useful) hobby tools on the market, such as Dremel power tools, punch and die sets, Optivisors, etc., only a few inexpensive essentials are needed to get started in the hobby. None of the following items cost more than a few dollars or pounds, which makes the initial investment probably the most economical of any hobby.

The most important item in any modeller's toolbox is the **hobby knife**. Although there are different types of knives, the cheapest and best in my view is the X-acto knife with replaceable blades. Hobby knives can be used to remove plastic parts from sprue or photoetch from its fret, to scrape away seam lines on parts, or to remove excess plastic or resin and nasty pour plugs. **Nail clippers** or small nail scissors are also a good alternative for performing some of these tasks.

A collection of different grades of **files** and **sandpaper** is also useful, and both are widely available at hobby stores and hardware outlets at minimal cost. **Nail files** are useful too, because they can simply be discarded once they become clogged with plastic or resin residue. It should be noted that filing and sanding does create considerable dust, and to avoid inhalation, it is also wise to purchase a **face mask** to cover your mouth and nose, particularly when sanding resin.

For me, one inexpensive yet vital accessory is a box of wooden **toothpicks** (the flat type). I use these to stir paint, to apply glue to tricky and hard-to-reach areas, to mix epoxy glues, and for many other needs, some of which will be covered in the chapters that follow.

Glues come in different forms, namely **plastic glue** (liquid or tube), **epoxy glue** and **cyanoacrylate** (also known as 'superglue'). Each of these is available in a variety of strengths, and should be handled with great care. Plastic glue is only effective on polystyrene kit surfaces, and works by melting and welding the surfaces together. Epoxy glues usually come in two parts, hardener and adhesive, which are mixed together when required. Epoxy glues are useful where you need a strong bond, such as between heavy white metal or resin parts. Cyanoacrylate

The ideal workbench: this one belongs to Paul Fraser, a good friend and fellow modeller. Paul has installed two overhead lights, and has all the tools within arm's length. Note his files on the magnetic strip across the shelf (very handy) and the safety mask. (CM)

No modeller ever has enough brushes! A wide assortment of varying sizes is essential. (CM)

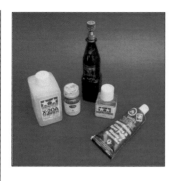

Other essential items: from left to right, Tamiya paint thinner for acrylics, Testors thinners for oils and enamels, a hand-held motor tool, liquid glue and modelling putty. (CM)

glue provides the ideal bonding agent for photoetch, smaller resin parts and plastics. Another bonus is its versatility: it allows you to bond different mediums to one another (i.e. resin to plastic, metal to resin, and so on.)

Epoxy putty is ideal for filling gaps or creating rough-textured surfaces, and once dry can easily be sanded, cut or shaped. Various hobby companies produce their own brands, including Squadron, Tamiya and Humbrol. Milliput is another brand popular among modellers. Epoxy putty designed for automotive body work is just as good as these hobby products, and you usually get more for your money. Look for it in hardware and automotive stores.

Brushes, airbrushes and paints

The finishing process is just as important as the construction of a model. The modeller has hundreds of **brushes** to choose from, with prices ranging from very cheap to the obscenely expensive. Brushes made from real hair are generally better than the synthetic type, and it is ideal to have five or six different sized ones, preferably as follows: '00', '0', '1', '2' and '3', a liner brush and a one-centimetre-wide flat brush.

As far as **paints** go, there are a few options open to the modeller. The two most popular types of paint are enamel and acrylic. Which type you use is a matter of personal choice, as opposed to one type being 'better' than the other, as both have their positive and negative aspects. Enamel-based paints (such as Humbrol, and XtraColour) tend to dry with a matt finish, are generally porous in nature, take longer to dry, and need to be mixed well before being applied. Acrylic paints (such as Tamiya, Vallejo and Gunze) dry in a matter of minutes, are relatively easy to work with (clean-up is minimal), but sometimes dry with a glossy or semi-glossy finish. As we shall see later, I prefer to switch between them depending on the specific purpose and effect required.

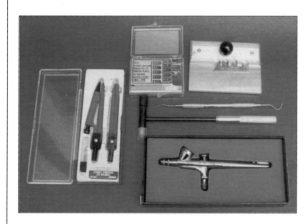

Non-essential items, but nevertheless very useful: from left to right, a compass, a punch-and-die set and mallet, Hold and Fold for bending photoetched materials, dental instruments for scribing, and an airbrush (this one is the Iwata HP-B). (CM)

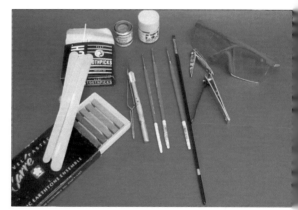

Other key items: clockwise from top left, toothpicks, paints, protective eye-wear, nail clippers, brushes of various sizes, a hobby knife, tweezers, pastel chalks, and emery boards. (CM)

Modelling the Matilda in small scale

Infantry Tank Mark I, A11 Matilda, 1/76 scale

Subject:	Infantry Tank Mark I, A11 Matilda, Royal Tank Regiment, BEF, France 1940
Model by:	Mark Bannerman
Skill level:	Intermediate
Kit:	A11 Matilda, Combat Ready series, Cromwell Models
Scale:	1/76
Additional detailing sets used:	None
Decals:	Stencils/Archer Fine Transfers
Paints:	Citadel Paints Primer (black)
	Testors Medium Green
	Vallejo Matt Black
	Vallejo Field Grey
	Polly S Railroad Grimy Black
	Humbrol Track Colour
	Various pastel shades
Wash:	Diluted Vallejo Matt Black

There are several reasons why I chose this subject. In the first instance, the A11 Matilda was a predecessor to the A12 Matilda, and despite the fact that the two tanks are dissimilar in almost every respect, the A11 and A12 together played a key role in the opening days of World War II with the British Expeditionary Force (BEF) in France. One tank cannot be mentioned or discussed without including the other. Secondly, small-scale modelling is growing fast in popularity. Thirdly, for this A11 model, I have opted to demonstrate a non-airbrush painting technique, and have placed the emphasis on using brushes and 'non-standard' techniques for the weathering process. The premise is that not everyone owns an airbrush or has immediate access to the more frequently discussed or described materials that one often reads about in magazines, manuals or on the Internet.

The kit chosen is a 1/76-scale A11 Matilda from the Combat Ready series by Cromwell Models of Scotland. These are highly desirable kits, and are particularly popular among collectors and wargamers. The kits are accurate, and are ideal for the first-time resin builder who may be apprehensive about working with this medium. Clean-up is minimal, assembly is quick and easy, and a modeller could conceivably build and paint a kit in one evening.

The kit comes in five sub-assemblies: two track sides with adjoined wheels, main body, turret and front plate. A sharp hobby knife was used to remove excess resin seams along the tracks, with sandpaper to smooth out a few rough spots. Don't forget to wear a mask when filing or sanding resin, and file or sand in a well-ventilated area: the dust can be hazardous to health. One tip is to wet the surface of the resin kit first, as this greatly reduces the amount of dust. Once all of the resin parts were cleaned up, I attached the parts with superglue and allowed this to dry for about 20 minutes. Make sure you remove any dust

Bovington Tank Museum's A11 Matilda in front view. (CS)

A rear view of Bovington's A11. (CS)

Side view of Bovington's A11. (CS)

specks on the surfaces that will be glued together, as dust particles can weaken the bond between joints. It is also better to apply glue to one of the surfaces, rather than applying it to both.

Once the glue had dried, I primed the kit. The reason for doing this is two-fold: primer provides the necessary 'key' for subsequent paint to adhere to, and it also provides a smooth, consistent finish, which allows you to spot small flaws or missed seam lines more easily. Primers can be purchased in many colours, but the recommended ones for armour are typically grey, black and white. If the vehicle is to be painted a dark colour (e.g. olive drab), black is best, while if it will have a lighter finish (e.g. dark yellow) a grey or white primer is advisable. Primer can be purchased in most hobby shops in aerosol-can form, or in small bottles for modellers who prefer to hand-brush or airbrush. For this project, I used an enamel-based paint in aerosol form from the Citadel Paints line, a type popular with Warhammer figure painters. It is smooth, consistent and relatively inexpensive. Both Testors and Tamiya also offer aerosol primer paints.

The primer was applied in two or three light coats, and left to dry overnight. The following day, I moved to the second stage, namely undercoating (sometimes referred to as 'basecoating'). Most modellers will use their trusty airbrush for this process, because an airbrush provides a more consistent and even finish, more versatility in the application and offers more possibilities for choice of colours. For the modeller without one of these, there are two options for applying the undercoat: by paintbrush, or by using ready-made paint mix through an aerosol can. I used both of these methods on the A11.

For the undercoat (or 'basecoat'), I chose a Testors colour from my local hobby store. Most armour colours are available in aerosol form: note, however, that it is virtually impossible to get an exact colour match, so a close match may be your only option. Moreover, the undercoat will change several shades with the subsequent treatments (to be covered later in this chapter).

My references for the A11's paint scheme described it as 'painted in a disruptive scheme of Dark Bronze Green applied by the troops in the field over a basic factory Khaki Green'. The Testors aerosol colour I chose was Medium Green, which was, in my opinion, a good match for the reference description of 'basic factory Khaki Green'. For the Dark Bronze Green disruptive scheme, I opted for Vallejo acrylic paint.

I applied the undercoat with two light sprays of Testors Medium Green, and allowed this to dry overnight. Two or three light coats are much better than one heavy coat, as the latter tends to obliterate fine detail.

For the disruptive scheme, I opted to handbrush the pattern using a mix of Vallejo Matt Black and Vallejo German Uniform Field Grey in a ratio of 3:1. Because this paint has very fine pigments, the dried paint will not leave any

Cromwell's kit has now been primed in three light coats using Citadel 'Chaos Black' from an aerosol can. The kit is ready for a base coat of green. (CM)

brush marks, resulting in a very smooth finish. The Vallejo acrylic paint is quite thick and should be diluted by adding a few droplets of water on a palette, along with a pea-sized drop of Field Grey and three pea-sized drops of Matt Black. A No. 2 round brush is ideal for applying the paint onto the Medium Green undercoat, because it allows more control over the amount of paint being applied in its application in tricky corners and on ridges, thus avoiding smearing the paint.

The acrylic paints took some 10 to 15 minutes to dry, and then a wash (usually, a diluted mix of thinners and paint – more tinted thinner than thinned paint) was applied to the surface of the model. The purpose of a wash is to accentuate and deepen the recesses on the kit's surface: the wash creeps (using capillary action) into all the nooks and crannies. The wash is applied in moderation and allowed to dry before another wash is applied. Most modellers use oil or enamel paints mixed with enamel thinners for the wash: for this particular project, though, I used Vallejo Matt Black paint mixed with water in a ratio of 1:6, and applied the wash with a 1cm-wide flat brush. The key to applying a wash is to be conservative with its application, and to apply three or four successive light washes rather than one heavy one.

Two light coats of Testors Medium Green from an aerosol can result in a smooth and even finish. (CM)

Once the base is dry, the process of laying down a darker camouflage scheme with acrylic Vallejo paints can begin. (MB)

The camo scheme was left to dry. The tracks were painted with Humbrol Track colour at this point too. A wash is then applied using a mixture of Vallejo paint diluted with tap water. (CM)

The next step was to paint the tracks and wheels. The wheel rubber was painted with Polly S acrylic 'Railroad Grimy Black' applied with a '00' brush: the tracks were painted with Humbrol Track Colour. The latter is hard to find sometimes, and an alternative is to mix black and brown (enamels or acrylics) in equal proportions and apply it in a very thin coat. I also applied the same colour to the muffler on the right rear of the tank.

The next stage was to add decals and markings. All the BEF's AFVs sported white squares on all sides to make the tank recognisable from any direction. A white number on a coloured square denoted a unit's position within a division, and was generally fixed to a metal plate on the front right side. The 4th Royal Tank Regiment painted on its tanks an eye in white with a black outline and blue pupil on either side of the upper turret. The A11 in France also carried a census number. For the white squares, I used stencils designed for architects, which are relatively inexpensive. Stencils are quite easy to use. Cut the stencil out, apply the front of the sheet to a piece of sticky tape, apply it to the surface and rub it down with medium pencil.

References indicate that the 1st Army Tank Brigade used a white '4' painted on a red square with a white line above to depict an army unit. This was made by carefully cutting out a very small square from sheet styrene, and spraying it with Tamiya Red from an aerosol can. A number '4' was taken from one of

The model is now dry-brushed with a lighter coloured enamel to accentuate the highlights. (CM)

The markings are applied with fine rub-on transfers. Note the results of the dry-brushing process on the rivets. (CM)

Archer Fine Transfers' excellent number sets. A larger number '1' from the same set served as the white horizontal line at the top of the square.

The eye on each side of the turret was an Archer Fine Transfers 'Ranger' from their figure shoulder patch set. I simply added the white around the existing blue inner section of the stencil with Vallejo paint. Lastly, I used Archer's number set for the census numbers.

The kit had a slight sheen to it, which I wanted to eliminate. I sprayed the kit with two light coats of Testors Dullcote in aerosol form. This muted the finish, as well as sealing the transfers on the surface of the kit. The Dullcote also slightly darkened the colours on the model.

The next step was to further accentuate the shadow areas using the pastel weathering technique, using artist's pastel chalks. These come in every conceivable shade, and are ideal for subtle details. Pastels are very versatile and can serve numerous purposes, as we will see later on. The pastels should be ground to dust using sandpaper or a nail file. The dust can then be applied with a brush (wet or dry) to areas requiring further enhancement and detailing. I filed down some black pastel, dipped my No. 1 brush into Tamiya thinner and then into the ground-up pastels, and applied the brush into grooves, shadowed areas and along joints and seams. The consistency of the mix should be similar to a wash, where there is more thinner than pastel. Dilute the pastels on a palette, and ensure that the mix is translucent, so that the palette can still be seen through the wash.

The pastel mix was applied to all of the joints and recessed areas, deepening the shadow area. This process can also be done using ground pastels without adding thinner – try both and see which one you prefer. In both instances, the pastels can be removed by applying a little Isopropyl alcohol or Tamiya Thinner, and rubbed them off with a brush or a cotton swab.

With the shadowed areas done, the highlighted areas also needed to be addressed, using dry-brushing. This technique requires a 1cm- or 2cm-wide brush (completely dry), an old rag and a little patience. The trick is to ensure the amount of paint on the brush is minimal: light strokes of the brush on the kit will deposit small amounts of paint on the raised points of the surface. For the A11, I chose Humbrol Khaki Green enamel mixed with a small amount of Titanium White from the Rembrandt oil paint line. The first step is to place a pea-sized amount of Khaki Green and the same of Titanium White on a palette: then I added a small amount of the white paint to the green, dipped my 1cm-wide brush into the mix, and scrubbed the brush on an old rag to remove most of the paint. I then stroked the brush lightly on the surface of the kit, flicking the brush rather than actually scrubbing it. The tips of the brush hairs should be the only part

Chalk pastels were filed to a powder and applied to all of the shadow areas to accentuate depth. With the pastels applied, the tracks and wheels were also weathered using enamels and pastels. (CM)

that makes contact with the kit's surface. Once the whole kit had received this treatment, I added a little more white to the green, and repeated the whole process. By the fourth or fifth dry-brushing application, the colour of the paint mix should be a very pale green, and a definite lighter colour should be apparent on the highlighted points of the kit.

When dry-brushing, there are a few tips to keep in mind. The brush should never be cleaned with thinners during the process, and the paints should not be thinned. It is also better to work through the process with too little paint on the brush than too much. If you reach a point where you think the kit requires just one more dry-brushing treatment, it is probably time to stop: it is better not to overdo it!

Last but not least, the final step in the weathering process is dusting and dirtying. Most modellers will use a combination of airbrushing and pastels chalks for this process. I chose to use a series of earth-coloured artist pastel chalks exclusively. I picked four different colours: Gold Ochre, Raw Umber, Burnt Sienna and Burnt Umber. I filed a small amount of each onto my palette and used a No. 3 brush to apply the dust in areas that would be exposed to dust and grime, such as the running gear, tracks, wheels and the front and rear vertical panels of the body.

This was a fun and enjoyable project that did not require enormous amounts of time to complete, and did not necessitate a huge investment in accessories and tools. Moreover, the techniques discussed in this chapter are equally applicable to larger-scale kits, as we shall see later on.

The base was made from two-part epoxy, some pastel chalks and a little dry-brushing. Note the dirt-like grime in the track treads. (CM)

Matilda Mk. III, Malta Tank Squadron, 1/76 scale

Subject:	Infantry Tank Mk. II, Matilda Mk. III, No.4 Independent Troop, Malta Tank Squadron, Royal Tank Regt. 1942
Model by:	Arthur Sekula
Skill level:	Advanced
Kit:	Fujimi
Scale:	1/76
Additional detailings sets used:	None
Paints:	Citadel Chaos Primer (black)
	Humbrol Matt White
	Humbrol Dark Yellow
	Vallejo Olive Drab Green
Wash:	Burnt Umber

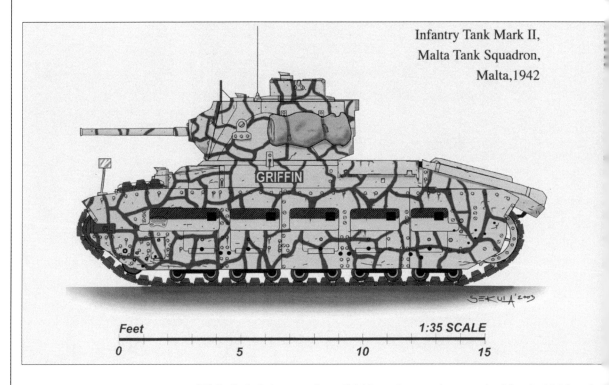

Infantry Tank Mark II,
Malta Tank Squadron,
Malta, 1942

GRIFFIN

SEKULA '2003

Feet   1:35 SCALE

0   5   10   15

Colour scheme and scale guide for the Maltese Matilda. (AS)

While little is known about British tank operations on the island of Malta, the Matilda did serve in small numbers on the island, primarily for airfield defence and as an armoured recovery vehicle. To better camouflage British tanks, crews typically applied sand-coloured patch patterns to their tanks and vehicles, in an effort to blend into the stone-walled terrain of the island.

Arthur Sekula, a Halifax-based graphic artist and avid modeller, decided to try his hand at the intricate and unusual Malta camouflage pattern on the Fujimi 1/76-scale kit. He built the kit out of the box with limited modification. The assembly was straightforward with little clean-up required, although some of the smaller parts suffered from misalignment of the halves. However, the detail was very crisp and the instructions were quite clear, making for an easy and enjoyable building project. There was, however, a substantial gap in the front between the

Note the small size of the Fujimi kit, shown here ready for primer. (AS)

An upper side view of the built kit. (AS)

lower and upper hull which required filler. Arthur used regular modelling putty to fill this gap, and once dry, he sanded the dried putty into shape. He also sculpted the missing front detail and hollowed out the main gun barrel, smoke-grenade discharger cups and turret hooks using a sharp hobby knife.

The kit was built before the paint was applied, including the tracks and running gear. Arthur primed the built kit with Citadel Chaos Black in two light coats, making sure the dark primer found itself into all of the shadows areas to help accentuate the crevices and the hard-to-reach areas on the surface.

The references show the Maltese Matilda had a sand-coloured undercoat with a dark linear pattern creating the stone shapes. However, it seems that, together with other tracked equipment used on the island during this period of the war, some Matildas arrived on Malta in their factory-finished Dark Khaki Green, while other Matildas were shipped from North Africa in an overall sand colour.

As there are so few pictures of the Maltese Matilda, and due to the poor quality of existing photos, it is difficult to deduce the way in which the colours and demarcation lines were applied to the tank. Some suggest that a dark brown colour may have been applied to a dark yellow base, while others think that tank crews simply 'painted on' the stone shapes, thus revealing the factory dark green base colour between the lighter areas. A further theory is that the dark yellow patches were painted on directly over the green factory base colour, and a black demarcation line was then applied to represent the space between the stone shapes. Since there is no hard evidence to prove any one of these theories right or wrong, it is possible that all of these methods were used. Arthur opted to keep the application simple and applied green colour lines on a dark yellow base.

After allowing the primer to dry thoroughly for a few hours, he applied a Humbrol base mixture of Matt White (22) and Dark Yellow (94) in a ratio of 1:3, using an airbrush. It is important to ensure that the paint is well thinned with an enamel-compatible thinner in a ratio of 1:1.

The kit was washed in soap and water. Once dry, it received two light coats of black primer, which was then left to dry for a few hours. (AS)

The kit has now been painted and weathered. (AS)

Left side view of the painted and weathered kit. Note the wash applied to the rivets along the track guard. (AS)

The exhaust pipe has been painted red-brown to denote rust. (AS)

A wash of Burnt Sienna adds another subtle depth of wear and tear to the model. (AS)

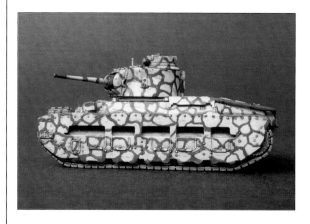

The addition of some light chipping and another wash completes the kit. (AS)

A rear side view. (AS)

Once the base coat of dark yellow was completely dry, Arthur proceeded to apply the dark green line pattern with Vallejo Olive Drab Green acrylic. The acrylic paint was applied with a little Windex window cleaner mixed in, to ease the flow of the paint onto the model, and to avoid undesirable brush marks. A number '000' brush was used to apply these fine lines: Arthur was careful to

The completed 1/76-scale kit added to a scenic base. (AS)

follow war-time photos of a Malta Matilda as reference for the style and shape. This process took approximately two hours to complete, and the model was then left to dry overnight.

Arthur then applied two light washes of Burnt Umber mixed with Taltine thinner in a ratio of 1:6 to help accentuate the shadow areas, and once dry, applied a light dry-brush of the sand-coloured base to highlight raised details. The dry-brushing helped to emphasise corners and edges where more wear would be apparent from the elements and from the crew. It also helped reduce the starkness of the green lines on the dark yellow base by blending the two colours together a little. It should be noted that adding washes to and dry-brushing small-scale models should be approached with caution: don't overdo it.

Arthur then proceeded to apply small scratches and nicks to the model, which would have been quite common for such a large tank travelling on narrow Maltese roads. For this he used finely-sharpened grey and silver artist's pencils. He also added some dust and dirt using sand-coloured pastel chalks. As a final touch, Arthur added a wire antenna and a side mirror to round off this project.

Small-scale gallery

Desert Matilda, 1/72-scale ESCI, by Rick Bennett

The assembly of the ESCI kit was quite straightforward, and Rick encountered only a few minor problems. The side skirts required a few 'dry fits' and some sanding before fixing with liquid glue. The tracks were too short, so Rick extended these by using sewing thread to connect the two ends and placed this section of track immediately behind the side skirts to hide the join. The gun barrel was replaced with brass tubing turned in a lathe. The smoke dischargers were also replaced with aluminium tubing. The exhaust outlets were hollowed out and additional tarps were added to the turret side stowage rack.

Once the kit had been assembled fully, the tank was airbrushed with a custom blend of Testors enamels. The decals were then applied using white glue mixed with water, which helped to create the painted-on look. Weathering was applied with diluted washes of Burnt Umber, Gold Ochre and Titanium White oils paints mixed with thinners. Details were then accentuated by carefully applying a controlled wash of Raw Umber to panel lines and underlying protrusions. To give the surface a bleached-paint look, Rick lightly dry-brushed over the surfaces with a small amount of neat white paint.

The groundwork, which consists of sand-blast dust mixed with acrylic gel, was brushed onto a wooden base. The Matilda was then placed on the groundwork, the Italian mile marker was added: finally, a little paint and dry-brushing completed Rick's vignette.

Side view of Rick's superb rendition of a Matilda on a scenic base. Note the careful attention to weathering of the bed rolls attached to the turret. (RB)

Frontal view of the ESCI 1/72-scale Matilda. (RB)

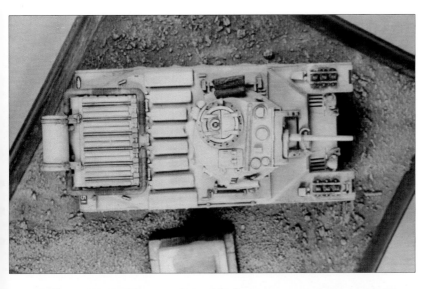

A light dry-brushing of white colour helps to create a dusty appearance. (RB)

Rear view of Rick's Matilda. (RB)

The scenic base helps to create the intended mood. (RB)

Modelling the Matilda in 1/35 scale

Australian Matilda Mk. IV 'Frog'

Subject:	Australian Matilda Mk. IV Frog 'Dangerous', 2/1st Armoured Brigade Recce Squadron, 4th Armoured Brigade
Model by:	Mark Bannerman
Skill level:	Advanced
Kit:	Tamiya (no. 35024)
Scale:	1/35
Additional detailing sets used:	MR Models Conversion (35146) Eduard photoetch (35099) Friulmodel tracks (ATL-72)
Decals:	Archer Fine Transfers
Paints:	Citadel Chaos Primer (black) Polly S Pullman Green Humbrol enamels 150, 100, 33, 72, 29, 83
Wash:	Rembrandt Sepia

Colour scheme and scale guide for the Matilda Frog. (AS)

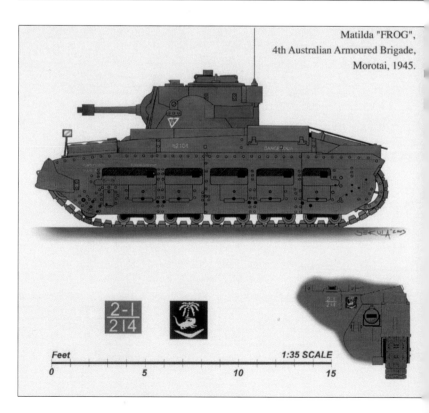

Matilda "FROG", 4th Australian Armoured Brigade, Morotai, 1945.

In the course of the fierce fighting around heavy Japanese fortifications in the Pacific, the Australian army converted some of their Matilda IV tanks to flamethrowers (nicknamed 'Frogs') to help eliminate enemy tunnel systems and strongholds. Although only 25 Matildas were converted in this way, they were

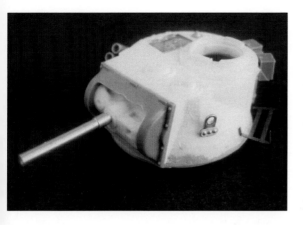

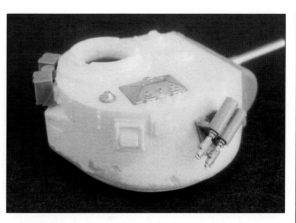

The MR turret with Tamiya and some Eduard photoetched parts added. (CM)

Note the pyramid-shaped loader's hatch – a unique feature often overlooked on the Matilda. (CM)

much feared by the Japanese, and saw heavy action in Tarakan and Balikpapan with the 2/1st Armoured Brigade Reconnaissance Squadron.

For this project, I used the Tamiya 1/35-scale offering, the MR Models conversion kit, the Eduard photoetch set, and Friul tracks. The MR conversion consists of resin and white-metal parts, as well as a turned aluminium barrel to depict the flame gun, with separate muzzle counterweight. The Eduard set contains some parts that would be needed for the project, and the Friulmodel tracks represent the correct 'spudded' type used by the Australians in the Pacific campaign.

The wartime conversion required replacement of the 2-pdr gun with a flamethrower, and fitting 80 gallons of fuel inside the turret. Additional flame fuel could be carried in other internal hull tanks and also in the jettison tank on the rear, but this was not common. The MR conversion provides a good rendition of the enlarged turret, and includes a splash protector around the gunner's periscope and the sunken screwheads that hold the circular turret roof plate. It also provides the raised pyramid edges on the upper surface of the loader's hatch flap, idler wheel guards, telephone box, low commander's cupola and PoW (petrol or water) tin carrier racks.

To start the construction process, the Tamiya kit turret was discarded and the MR resin turret cleaned up with a Dremel tool to remove the larger bits of carrier resin. Gunze Mr Surfacer was applied liberally by brush onto the turret to create a cast-metal effect evident on wartime photos of the Frog. The gun mantlet and metal barrel were fixed in place using superglue. Eduard photoetch was applied to the sides of the turret, and some of the Tamiya plastic kit parts were also added. Copper wire was added to the smoke dischargers and used for the grab handle on the loader's hatch. The hydraulic door rams were carefully glued in place and the antenna base was glued down.

As I was planning on adding a figure in the driver's compartment and commander's cupola, there was little need to detail the interior of the turret. The hull required some attention. The first step was adding the MR resin turret ring protectors. These are quite delicate, and were cleaned up with a nail file and fixed on with super glue. The two PoW can racks in the MR set were placed on both fenders and a thin strip of sheet styrene was added along the base of both racks. I made some rivets with a punch and die set, and added these along the inner front fenders using liquid glue.

Although the Tamiya kit requires some detailing and correction to the rear louvre area, I opted not to make any corrections. The reason for this is that I had planned on laying bomb-protection mesh over the louvres to represent the magnetic mine screens. This mesh was placed on the rear louvres by the crews to protect the area from enemy suicide charges. Different patterns existed, and the

A side view of the in-progress Frog. The turret has been placed on the Tamiya hull, and MR splash guards have been added. (CM)

A right side view. (CM)

Note the use of filler to plug holes. (CM)

The counterweight has now been added to the barrel, and the PoW (Petrol or Water) tin racks located on the fenders. The seams have also been added to the front with Evergreen rod. (CM)

material used was dependent on location and available materials. The simplest option for this conversion was the 2in. mesh type which I duplicated using regular screen door mesh. Other construction details included the reworking of the kit's exhaust pipes.

To finish the construction process, I added Grandt Line bolts on both sides of the tank to accommodate protection plates. My research revealed that Australian crews either welded tracks or protection plates onto the front and sides of their Matilda tanks, or used bolts to secure these in place. I opted for the latter by drilling out holes on both sides of the slanted hull, then laying the plates in place.

With all the details added and construction complete, it was time to start the painting and weathering process. At this point, the turret, upper and lower hulls were left unattached. The Friul tracks would be added later. For this project, I wanted to spend considerable time on the painting and weathering process by using several finishing techniques: pre-shading, post-shading, pin washes, wet pastel washes, and the 'filter' system.

First I primed the three sub-assemblies (turret, lower hull and upper hull) with Citadel Chaos Black, applied in two light coats by aerosol: the paint was left to thoroughly dry overnight. I then turned my attention to the tracks. The Friul T.D5910 tracks are an excellent replacement for the Tamiya vinyl offerings

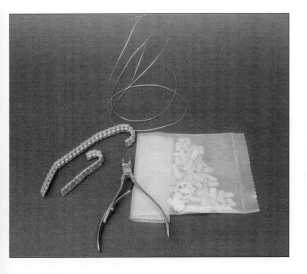

Friulmodel tracks are very easy to assemble and require little clean-up. (CM)

The rivets are added using a punch-and-die set. The commander's hatches are shown in the open position: these are fixed with superglue (cyanoacrylate). Note also that Eduard photoetched parts have also been attached. (CM)

Side track guard shields and front fender guards are added. The tracks are dry-fitted. (CM)

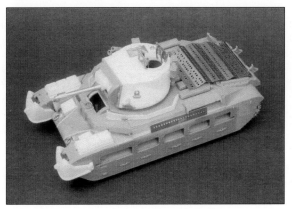

Top view of the completed construction stage. (CM)

The process of attaching the tracks requires pinning each link together with kit-supplied wire and adding a drop of superglue to keep the pin in place: it took the better part of two hours to put the tracks together. Although Friul tracks are advertised as 'left' and 'right' side, these are in fact all one-sided tracks. To remedy this, one can add a series of punch-and-die rivets on the exposed pin holes on the right side of the vehicle.

For the base painting of the tank, research revealed that Australian armour green was a darker tone than the usual British colours. I found a close match to be Pullman Green from Polly S, acrylic paints popular with railroad hobbyists. The paint was applied lightly in one coat to all three sub-assemblies through an airbrush, mixed equally with Tamiya thinners. I allowed this to dry for about an hour.

I attached the tracks to the lower hull, and glued together the lower and upper hulls using liquid cement. On the rear and front meeting points of the upper and lower hulls, I added a few dashes of superglue for extra strength. With the kit built, primed, its base colour applied, and the tracks fixed, I was ready to add a secondary base colour. However, here I encountered my first glitch. I received a very timely e-mail from an Australian contact informing me that Frogs typically

had orange-red fording lines across the track plates. Fording lines allowed the crew to determine the depth of rivers and swamps. So, I masked off the track plates with Tamiya masking tape, allowing two straight lines to show through on both sides of the tank. I sprayed two light coats of Humbrol Matt White and allowed this to dry overnight. The following day, I carefully hand-painted, using a liner brush, some Vallejo acrylic German Uniform Orange mixed with Napoleonic Red, making sure to keep my brush within the masking tape templates. I then peeled off the masking tape to reveal the fording lines. This was the only approach I could think of to apply these, short of stripping the kit of its primer and base paint and starting again.

For the markings, I wanted to depict a Mk. IV Matilda Frog, appropriately named 'Dangerous', serving with the 2/1st Armoured Brigade Recce Squadron, 4th Armoured Brigade. With the tremendous assistance of Michael Grieve in Australia, I managed to get hold of specific information on its markings. I used a variety of generic letter and number stencils from the Archer Fine Transfer series to apply the War Department numbers (82104), vehicle name 'Dangerous', and the 2/1st Armoured Brigade Recce Squadron arm-of-service sign (2-1 214) on the rear right plate and under the driver's hatch.

Once the markings were in place, I sprayed a light coat of ModelMaster semi-gloss clear to seal and protect the markings from subsequent weathering. I then proceeded with a secondary base colour using a mix of Humbrol Forest Green (150), Humbrol Matt Brown (100) and a hint of Matt Black (33) in a ratio of 10:2:1 (150/100/33). I also added Testors thinner to the paint in a ratio of 3:1 paint to thinner. This mix was airbrushed onto the kit in a fine mist and swirling cloud pattern at a 45-degree angle, allowing the paint to only settle on the top surfaces. This essentially produces a definitive lighter tone of green compared to the Pullman Green base, and greatly helped enhance the very dark (almost black) undertones in the shadow areas as a result of the initial primer. This very finely applied secondary base also helped reduce the starkness of the reddish-orange fording lines, as well as toned down the glossy appearance of the transfers.

For the weathering process, I began with a filter. This is a technique that helps break up the monotony of a single-colour paint job. I cleaned up my airbrush and prepared the filter paint mix of Rembrandt Sepia oil paint (10 per cent) with Humbrol thinner (90 per cent). I first sprayed the kit with straight thinner to break the surface tension, then added my filter mix to the airbrush

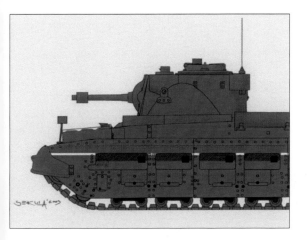

Stage 2: Add a light coat of Polly S Pullman Green acrylic paint mixed equally with Tamiya thinners. (AS)

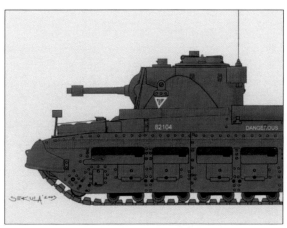

Stage 3: add the markings, and then spray on a light coat of ModelMaster semi-gloss clear to seal them. Then apply a secondary base colour with an airbrush, using a mix of Humbrol Forest Green, Humbrol Matt Brown and a touch of Matt Black. (AS)

Stage 4: apply a filter and pin wash, and then stipple the model with Humbrol Earth (29) to create dirt and mud effects. (AS)

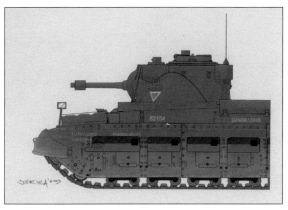

Stage 5: continue stippling, using Humbrol Matt Khaki Drill 72 blended with thinner. Finally, execute some subtle dry-brushing using light green enamels, and run a 2B pencil along the high-wear edges. (AS)

colour cup and re-sprayed the kit in a swirling pattern, making sure to cover the entire kit. Essentially, it gave a uniform, overall darker tone to the surface. I like this process because it goes a long way to making any subsequent washes blend with the surface colour.

When this had dried, I applied a technique called a pin wash – essentially a carefully placed wash, as opposed to an overall wash. The advantage is that it is controlled and manageable. I mixed Rembrandt Sepia (30 per cent) and Humbrol thinner (70 per cent) and began the task of applying the pin wash to all of the nooks, along seam lines and around bolts with a liner brush.

The kit was beginning to take on a definitive weathered look. In fact, the filter spray combined with the pin wash of the same Sepia colour changed the look of the model considerably. Although applying the pin wash was a tedious task, the results allowed for the surface to be kept intact and free of cat hairs and specks of dust, which is an inherent risk when doing overall washes. It also minimised any chance of the wash leaving 'tide marks', or nasty streaks of paint. The tank was left to dry for several days in a shoebox.

Two light coats of black primer are added, before a light coat of Polly S Pullman Green is applied with an airbrush. (CM)

At this point, I added the squadron and formation markings and the driver figure. As there are no existing decals of the Australian 4th Armoured Brigade formation sign depicting a palm tree, crocodile and boomerang, I handpainted the marking with a liner brush and white acrylic paint on a square background painted in black. I also affixed dry transfers identifying the squadron with an inverted Archer Fine Transfers equilateral triangle on both sides of the turret, with the number '6' inside the triangle to denote the troop to which the vehicle belonged.

I wanted to depict a fairly clean Frog that showed evidence of having been through swamps and rivers without completely obliterating the details of the tank. For this purpose, I concentrated my efforts on heavily weathering the lower part of the tank up to the red fording lines, and leaving the upper hull and turret relatively unsullied.

I used Humbrol Earth (29) to create the dirt and dried mud. The paint was poked and jabbed on the lower part of the side plate. I also mixed Humbrol 29 paint with some Testors thinner and ran my brush down from the track chute to denote seepage. I added Humbrol White to the Humbrol 29 and repeated the process to denote layered dirt.

The whole process was repeated using Humbrol Matt Khaki Drill 72 and I applied the paint in a jabbing motion using a dried-out brush. While the khaki was still wet, I blended the paint in a downward whisking motion to mute the starkness of the colour. I also added a little thinner to my brush and repeated the whisking motion until all of the earth-coloured paints had blended together. I also added some earth-coloured pastels sparingly to help blend the finish.

The next step was to execute a little dry-brushing. I dipped my brush in some Humbrol Matt Forest Green (150), rubbed the brush hairs onto a rag until almost all the paint was removed, and lightly brushed the surface of the kit in a whisking motion. I repeated the step, but added about 10 per cent Humbrol

The fording lines are added to the model's base, using masking tape and carefully brush-painting the red lines. (CM)

A few markings are added using Archer Fine Transfers. A light coat of Model Master semi-gloss clear seals and protects the markings from subsequent weathering. (CM)

The 4th Armoured Brigade formation sign depicting a palm tree and crocodile were hand-painted on using a liner brush. (CM)

A secondary base colour is now applied, using a mix of Humbrol Forest Green (150), Humbrol Matt Brown (100) and a hint of Matt Black (33) in a ratio of 10:2:1. This is lightly sprayed onto the model at an angle of 45 degrees. (CM)

Note the slightly lighter tone. (CM)

Next, a filter is added: the mix is made up of Rembrandt Sepia oil paint (10 per cent) with Humbrol thinners (90 per cent). This is applied using an airbrush. (CM)

Note how the model has taken on a darker, uniform tone. The squadron markings have now been added to the turret too. (CM)

Here the pin wash is being prepared, a mix of Rembrandt Sepia (30 per cent) and Humbrol thinners (70 per cent). (CM)

The pin wash is applied carefully and with moderation along seam lines, panel lines and around bolts, using a liner brush. (CM)

The first layer of mud and dirt is added by dabbing some thinned Humbrol Matt Dark Earth (29) along the outer edges of the shield, and creating streaks down from the shield vents with undiluted Humbrol thinners. Then a second, lighter application is applied, using Humbrol 29 again, but this time with a little Humbrol Matt White (34) added. (CM)

Note the light weathering on the track side shields. (CM)

The results of the mud weathering process after it has dried. (CM)

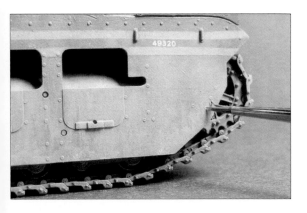

The same process was repeated with a larger brush using Humbrol Matt Khaki Drill (72), but this time only allowing the tips of the brush to touch the surface. (CM)

The layers are then blended together with a larger brush moistened with a small amount of thinners. (CM)

The results of the blending process after it has dried. (CM)

The exhaust pipes were painted in various dark-coloured Humbrol paints with artist's pastel chalks mixed in to give a textured finish. To depict asbestos tape, these were then wrapped in strips of pre-painted Tamiya tape cut to size. (CM)

The PoW (Petrol or Water) can rack mounted on the fenders. This was weathered with chalks mixed with Tamiya thinners. A silver pencil was run along the edges of the cans to represent a little wear and tear. (CM)

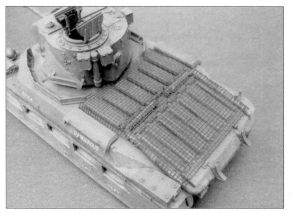

Door fly mesh was used to represent the protection mesh used by Australian crews. It was cut to size, bent and painted black. (CM)

A side view of the Frog. A tank commander has been added from the Hornet series. (CM)

The rear muffler was painted and weathered using the same technique as for the exhaust pipes: various dark-coloured Humbrol paints were mixed with powdered chalks to provide texture to the finish on the rear hull. (CM)

The driver is a combination of a Hornet head and an Ultracast body painted in the same manner as the commander. The shirt was painted in Humbrol 31 (Matt Slate Grey). (CM)

Matt Ochre (83) to the mix, and again repeated the light whisking motion. The process was repeated three to four more times, each time with an added 10 per cent of Matt Ochre. The final drybrush should be approximately a 1:1 mix of Humbrol 150 and Humbrol 83. The model was then left to dry for a day.

The exhaust pipes were painted in various brown coloured enamel paints mixed with chalks and applied with a large brush. I repeated the same process on the muffler on the rear of the tank using a mix of enamels and chalks. I then wrapped cut-down Tamiya tape to denote asbestos strips common to the Matilda tank. The tape was painted in Humbrol Slate Green.

I added the magnetic mine protection screen to the rear of the Frog using household fly-screen mesh cut to size and painted matt black. The rear jettison fuel tank included with the Tamiya kit was left off, as these were seldom fitted to the Frog. The armoured box on the rear left hull rear represents a tank infantry telephone, which was included with the MR conversion kit.

ABOVE The Frog was placed on a base made of two-part epoxy, a little static grass and painted in enamels. (CM)

BELOW The final product set against a suitable background photo added from a poster. (AS)

The finished model placed in a suitable 'Photoshop' setting. (UA)

I used a 2B pencil on all high-wear edges. The graphite colour looks exactly like steel, and by rubbing it gently with your finger tip, one can make the edges shine like exposed metal. Again, moderation is crucial – less is more.

The tracks were primed with Tamiya Dark Grey, and then airbrushed with a mix of Tamiya Flat Earth and Tamiya Flat Black. Once dry, they were washed with a mix of Raw Umber and Raw Sienna oil paint. I then brushed on dark brown pastel chalks mixed with Tamiya thinner. Once this had dried, the final step was to dry-brush the tracks with Humbrol Dark Earth (29).

I airbrushed the lower sides, lower bottom front and back of the model with Tamiya Buff mixed with Tamiya thinner (ratio of 1:5 paint to thinner) to create a dusty appearance. It is important to apply the paint in a work area with plenty of natural light, to ensure that the application is not too heavy. It can be very difficult to reverse if overdone.

For the finishing touches, I used an Ultracast figure for the driver and a Hornet figure for the commander, both with modified Hornet heads. The flesh tones were painted in Winsor Newton oils using a mix of Gold Ochre, Titanium White and Burnt Sienna, highlighted with added Titanium White and shadowed using Raw Umber. The shirts were painted in Humbrol enamels and shaded using Payne's Grey oil paint mixed with enamels.

Walk around a Frog

ABOVE A perfectly restored Frog at the RAAC Museum at Puckapunyal, Victoria, Australia. Note the red fording lines, as they would have appeared during the war. This Mk IV Matilda Frog carries markings of the 2/1st Armoured Brigade Recce Squadron, 4th Armoured Brigade. (MG)

The insignia of the 4th Australian Armoured Brigade. (MG)

The port side of the same Frog. (MG)

ABOVE A well preserved Frog housed at the Melbourne Tank Museum in Narre Warren, Victoria, Australia. The tank carries the markings of 2/1st Armoured Brigade Recce Squadron. (MG)

BELOW Note the yellow bridging sign denoting the weight of the tank, and the lack of headlights. (MG)

ABOVE Port-side front view of the Melbourne Tank Museum Frog. (MG)

BELOW This Frog is also to be found at the Melbourne Tank Museum. (MG)

ABOVE The rear view of the same tank on the bottom of page 37 with the exhaust removed. (MG)

BELOW A front view of the Frog. (MG)

Close up view of a Frog turret. (MG)

Close-up view of the cupola. There were two types: the early 'dustbin' type, and the later 'short' one. Nearly all Matildas had the 'short' cupola, which is 6in. high overall. (MG)

Close-up of the front idler guards. This is a one piece armour casting covering the tracks above the idler centre line, with a screw that allows for adjustment. (MG)

A close-up front view of the Frog's nozzle and counterweight. (MG)

A side view of the nozzle. (MG)

A close-up of the turret ring. The exact dimensions and location of the plates differed on individual tanks. (MG)

Rear view of the Matilda. Note the jettison tank mounting and the exhaust guard on the right. (MG)

The engine louvres of the Frog, onto which the crews would typically lay wire mesh screen. Note too the rough texture of the turret. (MG)

British Desert Matilda, 1941

Subject:	A12 Infantry Tank Mk. II, Matilda Mk. III, Western Desert, 1941
Model by:	Sean Dunnage
Skill level:	Advanced/master
Kit:	Tamiya (no. 35024)
Scale:	1/35
Additional detailing sets used:	Friulmodel tracks (ATL-71) Eduard photoetch set (35099)

Sean Dunnage based his Matilda on photos and drawings of various vehicles in the Western Desert during the war, and not on any particular tank. Although the Tamiya kit comes with the rubber band-style track, the detail is quite poor, and so a replacement set is essential. Sean chose the flat type track, most common on desert Matildas. The Friulmodel tracks are made of metal, and are pieced together using wire cut to length. It is not necessary to use the Eduard set in its entirety, as there are many items which are redundant or out of scale. In such cases, plastic sheet is preferable as a substitute for the photoetch parts.

Sean started his Matilda by assembling the lower hull. The weld seams at the front needed removing and all the holes on the bottom filled. Holes also needed to be filled where the exhaust system was to be mounted on the rear plate. All steps for the Tamiya build can be made up to Step 8 as illustrated in the instructions. Following with Step 9, the front idler wheels needed to be hollowed out so light could be seen through the spokes. The rear drive sprockets were replaced with the ones that come with the Friulmodel track set. At this point, the sand chutes and support rollers can be added to complete the lower hull.

If the modeller plans on an interior, this would be the time to add the internal bulkheads and remove all of the motor mounts that are cast into the lower hull. The interior was built using mostly sheet styrene, many parts from a spares box, various leftover photoetch from other kits and putty. Reliable interior photos are essential: Sean's references were Osprey's New Vanguard 8 *Matilda Infantry Tank 1938–45* and materials from the AFV Interiors website.

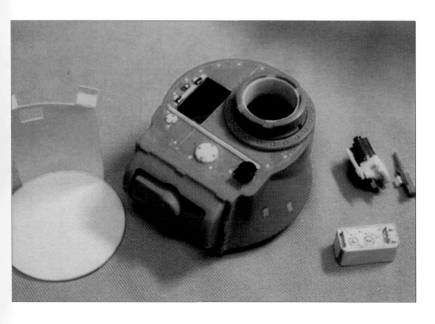

Reworking the turret using sheet styrene. (SD)

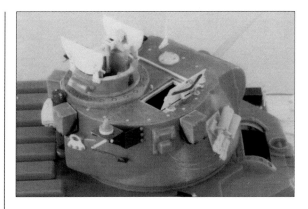

The reworked turret. Small copper wire, photoetched parts, sheet styrene, resin and bits from the spares box make for a very impressive looking turret. Note the carefully placed rivets and the high level of detail in the interior. (SD)

Left side view of the turret. Note Sean's use of putty to plug up holes and smooth out surface detail. He has also added the exhaust pipes and the rear Friul sprocket. (SD)

The detailed interior. It is essential to find reliable interior photos for reference. (SD)

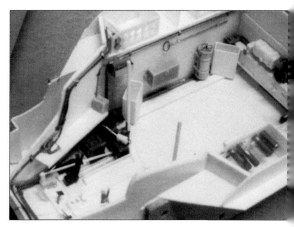

Sheet styrene was drilled out to accommodate the 2-pdr shells. Various gauges of soft copper wire were used in the interior to depict wire and cables. (SD)

The upper hull required some work to accurately depict a Matilda. The first step was to remove approximately 1mm from the angled sloping armour which is located on both sides of the driver's hatch, and replace it with sheet styrene. When looking at the model from above, the angles of this armour are far too exaggerated when compared with the real tank. Next, the weld seams were filed down, as the welds are both in the incorrect place and not at the correct angle. At this stage, one needs to decide if the two compartments located behind the headlights will be shown with the vents as per the Tamiya model, or closed over with steel plate. Sean chose the latter option by using sheet styrene. Vent covers were added by many Matilda crews, as it was found that items in the compartments had a tendency to catch fire when hot shrapnel found its way through the vents. Sean also thinned the fenders with sandpaper to bring these to their proper thinness.

Moving to the rear deck, Sean removed the moulded-on hinges around the engine louvres and replaced these with short sections of plastic rod. Once complete, the louvres were added, using plastic card to represent missing details. The two outermost louvres needed to have a section of rod added to show the hinge that runs along the outer edge just underneath.

The upper hull required considerable work, including sanding down inaccurate parts and adding putty where it was necessary (for example, to the nose area). (SD)

Note the replacement of new rivets along the upper track guard. (SD)

Sean blanked over the two holes in front of the louvres where the exhaust pipes would be fitted. The reason for this is that he made his exhaust pipes using thick 'plumber's' solder, which is not the same size as the kit parts. Therefore, blanking these over provided room for error in the placement of the new pipes, and covered any gaps. All placement holes on the hull were filled with putty and sanded down. Deck details were added with small latches at the rear of the engine deck using plastic rod and sheet plastic. The fuel-tank mounts were added using sheet styrene, and the rear tow-hook links were glued in place. Sean also used some square plastic stock and kit parts to replace the Tamiya mounting brackets. Several bolt heads were added on the rear fenders.

The rear-light assembly was then added, located on the right rear fender. Many photos show this item missing, presumably through damage or wear and tear. If the modeller opts to leave this detail off, make sure to leave three small holes where the assembly would be bolted.

Moving forward on the right side of the hull, Sean added a shovel from the Tamiya Cromwell kit and a pick handle. These items were secured using parts

ABOVE The fuel-tank mounts were added using sheet styrene, and the rear tow-hook links were glued in place. (SD)

ABOVE All placement holes on the hull were filled with putty and sanded down. Small deck details were added, such as the small latches at the rear of the engine deck made from plastic rod and sheet plastic. On the front of the hull, Sean added a shovel and a pick handle. These items were secured using parts from the Eduard set and from the spares box. (SD)

ABOVE A rear view of the assembled model. (SD)

from the Eduard set and from the spares box. The straps are simply lead foil with photoetch buckles. To the right of these items on the sloping armour a large crowbar would usually be located. This was left off, but the bracket was attached using photoetch. On the left side of the hull, Sean added an antenna stowage case. This was made by flattening out a round copper tube and adding a strip of half round to the top. Again, the mounting brackets are from Eduard and the spares box.

Moving up to the front, there is the driver's vision port: the opening was drilled out and the kit's visor added. The sidelight protector boxes located on the left and right fenders were replaced with the Eduard offerings and plastic rod was used for the two protection arms located just in front of the boxes. The spare track brackets are simply flat plastic stock cut to size and three spare links from the Friulmodel track set were added. The right front fender holds a mirror bracket. Sean chose to only add the bracket, not the mirror.

Most photos depicting wartime Matildas show the mirrors removed. For the headlights, there are several options. One can use the Tamiya offerings, as these are standard blackout lights found on most military vehicles throughout the war. Or, one can hollow out the lights and add aftermarket lenses. Tank crews would turn the lights around so that they would be facing the hull, which would have helped prevent them from being damaged in battle and, more importantly, stop any reflection that would give away the tank's position to the enemy.

Wiring for the lights is not necessary, as the wires run through the light mounting brackets. One could also use some lead foil and cover the headlights, making it look like a canvas cover. The front tow hooks were replaced using spares from the parts box and some scratchbuilt plates using plastic card and Grandt Line bolt heads. Looking closely at wartime pictures will help with both placement and sizing.

At this stage of assembly, one can put the upper and lower hulls together. The front of the tank requires new weld seams. Sean made them by soaking plastic rod in liquid cement to soften the rod and then placing these in position. This method is extremely effective, because these would naturally be rough in texture. Small cuts are necessary where the welds jump the front stowage bins. This cut is directly in line with the hinges.

Moving to the rear of the hull, Sean added scratch built mufflers. The kit items can be used, but he used brass tube cut to length, and then plugged both ends with plumber's putty. Once sanded flat, .005-sized plastic card was wrapped around the brass tube, leaving about 1mm protruding from the ends to give the necessary indentation. Small kit exhaust outlets were added. The brackets holding the mufflers together were made using square plastic stock and sheet brass.

The exhaust pipes leading from the engine to the mufflers were then added. These pipes are made from thick 'plumber's' solder that is easily bent and formed to the correct angles. Matilda exhausts seem to vary in style, and Sean chose a more elaborate version, which has heat protection wrapping added to them. He took soft copper wire and wove it around the pipes, gluing it in place as it was wrapped, then added some lead foil to several points showing the pipe connections.

The brackets holding the exhaust pipes to the tank are plastic card cut and bent to shape. For the final touches to the rear hull, Sean added some missing bolt heads and plates. The external fuel tank was then added and a fuel line from the tank to the engine was made using electrician's solder. Two handles were added using bent brass wire. The straps holding the fuel tank to the brackets that mount the assembly to the tank are cut from thin brass sheet, which is cut to size once applied. For a final detail, Sean added an Ultracast rack of 'flimsies' to the right rear skirt.

Following his references, Sean cut out a hatch so that the left side of it is running with the horizontal line scribed earlier. The hatch itself can be made of sheet plastic, and hinges added using the same material. Details can be added to the hinges using Grandt Line bolt heads. The hatch rest was made using both a spare piece from an old photoetch set and some plastic rod. Again, the handle was copper wire bent to shape, and the padlock clasp was taken from an old Aber set. The small piece of angle running across the diameter of the turret is from Evergreen Scale Models. The lifting rings located at three points on the Matilda are made from scratch. The tarp rack is made from plastic strips and modified slightly so as to have a bit more of a curve to match the contour of the turret. Eduard photoetch was used for all three boxes located around the top of the turret, and also for the antenna mount. Sean added a piece of coiled wire to look like the spring, which is located just underneath the mount. The small tube located just behind the commander's cupola is meant to hold the signal flags that the British used when radio silence was in effect. This was replaced with a home-made copper tube and lead foil.

For the commander's cupola, Sean replaced the kit hatch covers, which are too thick and lack detail. If you opt to keep these closed, only a cover needs to be added to the periscope. If you decide to leave the hatches open, pistons that help the commander to open and close them need to be added. The pistons were made using some plastic rod of varying diameter. The search-light was replaced with a scratchbuilt item using sheet styrene and some old photoetch. Sean also added the handle located in the cupola that is used to direct the light. The final major turret detail tackled were the smoke dischargers (mastered by Sean for Maple Leaf Models) located on the right side of the turret. The wires leading to the dischargers are made from fine brass wire

ABOVE British vehicles used both a Caunter scheme and a solid pattern style of camouflage, so the choice of finish is at the modeller's discretion. Sean sprayed a base of sand colour over the entire assembly, using Tamiya Dark Yellow XF-60 and Khaki XF-49. (SD)

ABOVE Sean chose to depict a relatively new tank, so weathering was kept to a minimum. Here we can see the areas of general wear and tear around the turret. (SD)

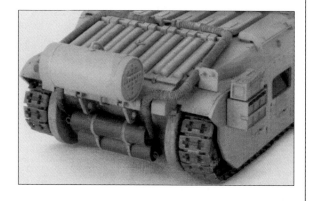

ABOVE Detail of the rear of the finished model. The tracks were painted using Tamiya Gun Metal X-10, and then were highlighted with a dry-brushing of silver. (SD)

A port-side view of the painted Matilda. (SD)

Starboard-side view of the completed model. (SD)

and threaded through the right side pistol port. Many photos show this as being the most common method used with this style of discharger. To finish off the turret, Sean added some final bits from the Eduard set and a tarp made from plumber's putty, which was fitted to the rack while still pliable.

The Matilda has a fairly rough finish to it, which is left by the casting process, and Tamiya has omitted this detail. To accomplish the 'cast' look, Sean applied a generous amount of liquid cement all over the tank, then stippled it using a short stiff paintbrush. Another method of creating this look is to apply Gunze Sangyo Mr Surfacer, and then stipple it.

The Friulmodel tracks were assembled and placed between the side skirt and the hull. For the painting process, Sean removed the tracks. Finally, personal equipment, helmets, bedding and packs were added.

According to a Middle East General Order, the colours of the Caunter scheme by area were officially a Light Stone (British Standard Colours 61) base colour plus stripes of Silver Grey (BSC 28) and Slate (BSC 34) in Egypt, or Light Purple Brown (BSC 49) in the Sudan: other shades may have been used as available though. The darkest shade was always the top colour and covered most of the vehicle seen from above: from the side, the balance of light and dark was supposed to be equal. There was also a later scheme using just two shades, which can be mistaken for the true Caunter scheme. Sean elected to paint his Matilda using desert sand, slate grey and pale green.

Sean gave the model a wash with warm soapy water to remove any dust and debris that had become attached to the model during the building process. At this stage, the turret, hull and tracks were all separate. Once the model had dried, he sprayed a base sand colour over the entire assembly with a 4:1 mixture of Tamiya Dark Yellow XF-60 and Khaki XF-49. This mixture was then thinned 20 per cent using Tamiya Thinner X-20A. Once the sand base had dried for 24 hours, he masked the tank with 3M Scotch tape. The first colour to be applied was slate blue. This colour is made up of Tamiya Neutral Grey XF-53 and Flat White XF-2, mixed in a ratio of 1:3 with 20 per cent thinner added for spraying. The Tamiya acrylics dry quickly, and the masking should be removed about 10 minutes after spraying. Sean then applied masking for the final colour of the Caunter scheme, pale green, for which he used Model Master RAF Interior Green #2062 enamel thinned by 40 per cent.

The tracks were painted using Tamiya Gun Metal X-10, then highlighted with a dry-brushing of silver. Once the tracks had dried, Sean added these to the model. The exhaust system was painted with a mix of rust and gunmetal, which gives the system a metallic feel. The pipes on the upper deck were painted with a heavily-thinned rust colour, so that it would flow around the outer wrapping of the system and not affect the colours of the Caunter scheme.

Weathering was kept to a minimum. Sean added chipping around the hatches where the crew would climb in and out of the vehicle. The sand chutes also received small chips using a base colour of Tamiya Olive Drab XF-62 with a touch of Flat Brown XF-10, applied with a No. 2 brush. Sean then sprayed the entire model with a gloss coat to prepare it for a wash of thinner with Burnt Sienna oil paint. Once the gloss was applied, tank registration numbers were added, then sprayed again with gloss to seal them in. The wash was applied using a wide flat brush. Once it had dried (after a week), Sean used graphite powder to show wear on the tank where the crew would most frequently walk or slide around, and to show where the sand had run down the chutes. The kit was given a coat of semi-gloss to seal everything in and to help blend the weathering. Sean's headlights are actually dolls' eyes, which can be bought in any craft store. He cut the backs off and added a piece of tinfoil for reflection. The searchlight lens is from the Greif line, and was simply glued into place. Even though Tamiya's Matilda is relatively unsophisticated, it is possible to create a very nice model from the kit with a little patience and a few aftermarket accessories.

ABOVE Another stunning piece of artwork by Ron Volstad, showing a Matilda desert tanker in typical dress.

1/35 gallery

'Arras' A12 Matilda, by Steve Zaloga

Steve Zaloga is world-renowned for his many fascinating and unusual conversion projects, dramatic vignettes and his meticulous attention to technical and construction detail. Here, Steve has provided a superb reworking of the Tamiya kit to depict an early production version of the Matilda with the BEF in France in 1940. Considerable work was done to correct the kit's inaccuracies at the outset, and careful reworking was carried out to backdate the kit to an early version Matilda using sheet styrene, photoetch and parts from the spares box.

The alterations and modifications to the hull area were considerable and included reworking the driver's hatch and increasing the angle inwards by adding sheet styrene, extending the half-round trim upward from the glacis plate, and removing the kit trim on the stowage door hinge and smoothing this out with sand paper.

A close-up of the detailed work on the turret of Steve's Matilda. There were numerous modifications to the kit's turret, including the addition of a pyramid-shaped hatch made from sheet styrene. The alterations and modifications to the hull included reworking the driver's hatch and removing the kit trim on the stowage door hinge. (SZ)

The front of the Matilda. The mudguards on the front and the rear were built up from sheet styrene. (SZ)

Steve also lowered the entire suspension by increasing the running gear's ground clearance. This was achieved by remounting the assemblies below the kit's location sockets – a small but important detail for the BEF Matilda. Steve notes that this results in the kit tracks not being long enough. However, because the tracks are partially hidden, these were cut and pinned in place. Other modifications to the suspension included thinning the edges of the bogie frames, and correcting the idler wheel mounting. Steve indicates that during test trials before its first appearance in France, there were concerns that the Matilda would become trapped in trenches. Therefore, all the Matildas were subsequently fitted with a tail skid to prevent the tank from sliding into them. Steve built his tail skid from sheet styrene, using various photos from German sources for reference.

Because the early Matildas in France were equipped with AEC engines and only had one exhaust pipe, Steve also reworked the upper deck by filling holes on the engine deck and replaced the exhaust pipe with aluminium rod. Mudguards on the front and rear were built up from sheet styrene, rivets were

Before the tank's first appearance in France, all the Matildas were fitted with a tail skid. (SZ)

Upper view of the kit with construction completed. (SZ)

ABOVE The model was placed on a scenic base, featuring static grass, and a suitable background was added. (SZ)

BELOW Prior to applying paint, Gunze Sangyo Mr Surfacer 500 was applied in several coats to fill in small gaps, as well as to create some cast texture. A Wolf resin figure was used for the tank commander. (SZ)

ABOVE For the finish, Steve chose a two-tone green scheme for his Matilda. First, he airbrushed the kit with Tamiya Khaki Drab, then Vallejo acrylic Deep Bronze Green was applied by hand. (SZ)

Note the subtle dusting and weathering on the rear. Steve applied Windsor-Newton acrylic gel to the sides to depict textured dirt, then airbrushed earth colours on the lower section of the tank, finishing the weathering off by carefully applying a wash of a mineral spirits mixed with raw umber oil paint. (SZ)

A view of Steve's superb Matilda from the top. (SZ)

applied in all areas as indicated by reference photos, and Eduard photoetch was used to correct several of the kit's smaller inaccuracies (such as adding spare track racks).

Steve carried out many modifications to the kit's turret. Locator holes were plugged, roof fittings removed, sunken roof panel bolts added with a Dremel tool, Ultracast's 2-pdr gun barrel was added, and smoke mortars using plastic tubes were fitted. The kit's right hatch was incorrect, and so Steve built a triangular-shaped hatch from sheet styrene.

Prior to applying paint, several coats of Gunze Sangyo Mr Surfacer 500 were applied to fill in small gaps and to create 'cast' texture. Appropriate markings were added using dry transfers on clear decal sheets. Steve painted his BEF Matilda in a two-tone green scheme. The kit was first airbrushed in Tamiya Khaki Drab and then Vallejo Deep Bronze Green acrylic was applied by hand.

The weathering process included the application of Winsor-Newton acrylic gel to the sides to depict textured dirt (this was done prior to the base paint being applied), and airbrushing earth colour on the lower section of the tank followed by careful washes of a mineral spirits and Raw Umber oil paint mix. Once dry, some dry-brushing was carried out, followed by the application of artist's chalk pastels.

A modified Wolf resin figure was used for the tank commander: Resicast provided the Vickers gun team. All heads were replaced with Hornet offerings. The heads were painted using oils paints, and the uniforms were painted in acrylic paints. The project was them mounted on a scenic base featuring static grass and suitable backdrop was provided for the photography. Steve's conclusion is that 'overall, this was a pleasant project that results in a model that looks very different to the desert Matilda'.

Desert Matilda Mk. III, 7th RTR, by Juan L. Mercadal Pons

Juan Luis Mercadal Pons is a modeller from Spain who won a bronze medal at the AMT show, a silver medal at Almería 2002 and a silver medal at S'Estel for this Matilda.

For his depiction of the 'Queen of the Desert', Juan used the Tamiya offering, which as we have already seen is rather old and in need of attention – but the general dimensions are good, and it is the only kit of its type on the market. The construction began by eliminating all the protruding details and replacing these with photoetch from Eduard, parts from the spares box, and sheet styrene and putty. Particular attention was given to reworking the idler wheel supports, the mudguards, the drag hooks, the exhaust pipes, and details on turret.

Major work included the addition of front fenders using plastic card, the addition of weld seams on the front hull, creating cast-texture using putty and liquid glue, as well as adding rivets throughout the tank to ensure accuracy. Juan also heavily reworked the turret using photoetch, plastic card, and copper wire. The kit's exhaust pipes at the rear were replaced using aluminium rod bent into shape, which were then wrapped in thin strips of Tamiya tape to represent the asbestos protection.

For the painting process, Juan applied the three-colour Caunter scheme (Portland Stone, Silver Grey and Slate or Medium Bronze Green) using Tamiya paints and tape to keep the lines consistent. He worked by painting from light to dark colours. Tanks of the 7th RTR took on names beginning with the letter 'G (being appropriately the seventh letter in the alphabet) and so this was followed in the markings.

The turret on Juan's Matilda was reworked with photoetched brass, copper wire, and sheet styrene and a turned barrel was added. (JM)

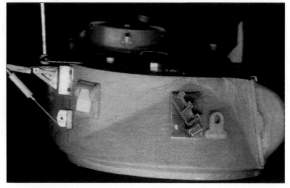

A close-up view of the turret's side. (JM)

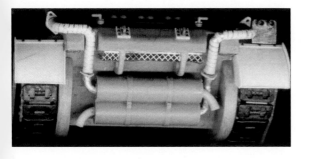

The exhaust leading to the muffler was replaced with soft rod, which was bent to shape. It was then wrapped in Tamiya tape to represent the asbestos tape. (JM)

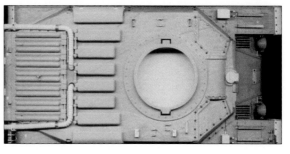

An upper view of the completed body. Juan added grey putty to create a textured surface. (JM)

RIGHT Front view of Juan's finished Matilda. (JM)

CENTRE A top view of the Matilda.

BOTTOM The Matilda was finished in the three-colour Caunter scheme, comprising Portland Stone, Silver Grey and Slate or Medium Bronze Green. Juan used Tamiya paints and masking tape to create this. (JM)

ABOVE Side view of the Matilda. (JM)

BELOW Rear view of Juan's completed model. Note the textured effect on the muffler and the heavy weathering on the side track guards using subtle washes and drybrushing. (JM)

Scratchbuilding a German Matilda 'Oswald'

Subject:	Infanterie Panzer Mk. II 748 (e), 'Oswald'
Model by:	Mark Cooper
Skill level:	Master
Kit:	Tamiya (35024)
Scale:	1/35
Additional detailing sets used:	Elefant 5cm barrel
Decals:	Archer Fine Transfers Balkencruz
Paints:	Vallejo Neutral Grey (992), German Grey (995), and Black Grey (950).
	Humbrol Matt Gull Grey, Matt White, Matt Earth (26), Matt Khaki (77) and Matt Ochre (88).
	Tamiya Neutral Grey XF-53, Buff XF-57, and Matt Black.
Wash:	Raw Umber
	Burnt Sienna

Colour scheme and scale guide for the Oswald. (AS)

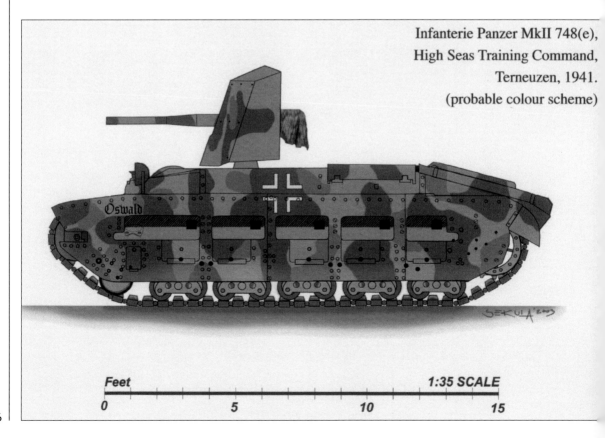

Infanterie Panzer MkII 748(e),
High Seas Training Command,
Terneuzen, 1941.
(probable colour scheme)

Oswald

Feet

0   5   10   15

1:35 SCALE

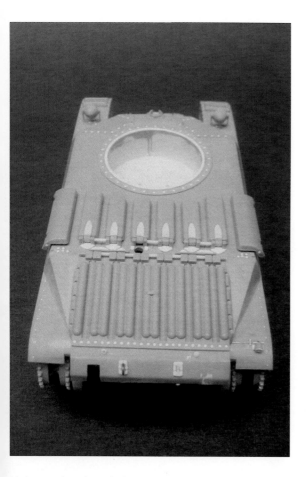

The interior fighting compartment is made from sheet styrene cut to shape and inserted in the turret area. (MC)

Mark started work on the louvres by adding some latches made out of sheet styrene. (MC)

Mr Gunze Surfacer was used to provide texture to the front hull. Also, kit rivets were removed and replaced with new rivets using a punch-and-die set. (MC)

Mark Cooper is a world-class modeller with an interest in building obscure and unusual variants which are ill-provided for in terms of after-market products. Mark prefers to use materials that are easily accessible, as will be shown in this chapter, and much can be accomplished using the most basic of materials combined with patience and solid research. For his project, Mark used the Tamiya 1/35-scale Matilda, sheet styrene, strip and rod, brass strip and rod, copper wire, Tamiya tape, aluminium foil and an Elefant 5cm L/42 barrel. Given that a number of short-comings on the Tamiya Matilda have been addressed previously, this chapter will focus on the detailing Mark added and his methodology.

The subject in question is a captured BEF Matilda in German service. There is little information available on these vehicles, their use and their fate, but Mark's interest was aroused after spotting a photo of one of these captured Matildas in a reference book. Using other references in his library, Mark was able to compile four photos showing at least two different tanks, both with the name 'Oswald'. The reference photos were taken at the High Seas Training Command based at Terneuzen on the Scheldt estuary.

The first step in the construction process comprised laying out the kit sprues and instructions and comparing these with Mark's reference material. The Tamiya Matilda is an old kit designed for motorisation, and as such, there are numerous mistakes and areas that need attention: a checklist divided into the various sub-assembly sections is very handy at this stage. The front hull of the Matilda is supposed to be cast (Tamiya's Matilda is without texture) so Mark

Rivets were added by carefully measuring the space between each one and adding a mark with a pencil. Mark re-riveted the entire upper hull. (MC)

Extra details were added to the front of the model. The headlamps are shown here in place. (MC)

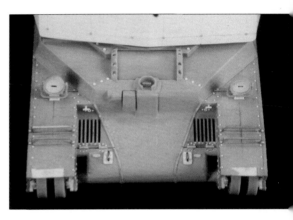

The front headlights were moved by the Oswald's crew and relocated on the fender. (MC)

An overall view of the detail added to this area of the kit. (MC)

added multiple coats of Gunze Mr Surfacer. This lacquer-based filler was applied with a cheap paintbrush that was discarded after the project. He applied very light coats and stippled the surface, not allowing the previous coat to dry completely: in this way, he was able to build up a very realistic finish, which took about 20 minutes to achieve.

Tamiya's Matilda is also too wide in the upper front hull: this is easy to correct by cutting away the sides and replacing it with sheet styrene. However, Mark elected simply to thin down the section by first using a razor saw, and finishing off with an assortment of files and sandpaper. The plastic in this area is almost 2mm thick, so there is some room to work with, and the end result is close to the actual measurements.

The upper rear hull of the Matilda provides access to the engine compartment and oil coolers: on the real vehicle the various panels are hinged. The Tamiya detailing is very crude, however, and Mark carefully chiselled away the details and rebuilt the area using styrene strip and rod, a job which took a few hours to complete.

Just as Steve Zaloga had done, the suspension was lowered in order to increase the ground clearance of the vehicle by mounting the running gear on the hull just below (about 2mm) the designated area shown in the instructions. In doing so, the running gear became more visible, and it was necessary to add additional detail to the running gear in the form of a bolt to the middle of each bogie. Since Mark did not have a supply of hexagonal bolts to hand, he took the necessary details from the inside of each bogie by shaving off one bolt from each with an X-acto knife.

In common with many early tank designs, the British made extensive use of rivets on the Matilda. A punch-and-die set was used not only to add new rivets and screws, but to replace rivets removed during the clean-up and conversion phase. In this case, photographs of the Aberdeen Proving Grounds Matilda proved to be invaluable.

For the rivets on the hull, Mark marked out the location with a pencil and glued each rivet in place with a small mount of liquid glue on a fine-tipped paint brush. The screw heads were applied in a similar manner, and once the glue had set, Mark went back with a clean X-acto blade and cut each rivet in half.

The track tensioner is a fairly prominent feature on the Matilda, but Tamiya neglected this particular detail entirely. Fortunately, it is a fairly basic detail that can be constructed using an assortment of styrene strip and rod. The only challenge was sourcing the hexagonal nuts, and in this case Mark turned to fellow modellers to supply the necessary materials. With the addition of this detail it was impossible to use the kit's idler mount (part B3), so the mounting hole was filled in and the idler was mounted between the tensioner using a small piece of brass rod.

As depicted in the reference photographs Mark repositioned the headlights on the front fenders. While working on this particular aspect of the kit, he added a few minor details in the form of a mounting bracket made from styrene and electrical wire, along with brackets made of brass wire and heavy aluminium foil. He also replaced the kit's spare track holder with new brackets fashioned from brass strip. Brass strip is readily available at most hobby shops and easy to work using pliers, wire cutters and files.

A close-up view of the turret basket, which was scratchbuilt using sheet styrene. (MC)

Photos of the converted Matilda unfortunately do not show the turret basket, so Mark constructed a very basic basket using an assortment of sheet styrene and tread plate. Once the mount for the kit's turret had been removed, the turret basket's floor was cut using a circle cutter and the walls were formed using .005 styrene sheet. He estimated the depth of turret basket using a 1/35-scale figure as a gauge and comparing the model to one of the photos showing the tank's gunner.

Mark made a few small modifications to the Matilda's exhaust that really improved the look of the stock parts. The muffler pipe was lengthened and strips of Tamiya tape (approximately 2mm wide) were wrapped around the exhaust to recreate the asbestos insulation and secured with a small amount of glue.

The construction of the gun shield was a relatively easy process using sheet styrene. Mark determined the approximate size by measuring the photographs and converted the measurements to match the Tamiya hull. A template was made with cardboard. Once he was satisfied with the general dimensions, the parts were cut out of sheet styrene. Setting and maintaining the proper angles while the glue dried was accomplished through the use of strips of styrene on the inside of the gun shield, an assortment of model clamps and a steady hand.

The barrel, breech and gun mount were the most difficult part of the project. Since Mark was unable to

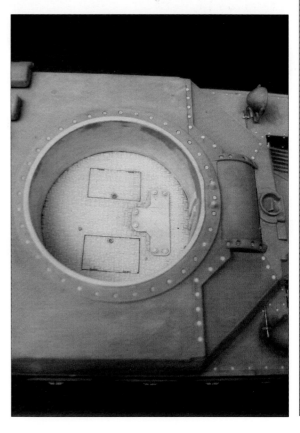

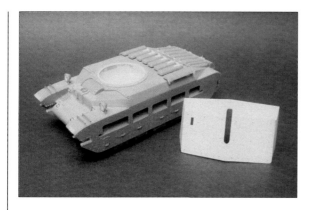

The front shield was built using sheet styrene following careful study of wartime photos to ensure correct scale. (MC)

The inside of the shield. (MC)

The breech was scratchbuilt, and has an Elefant barrel added to it. (MC)

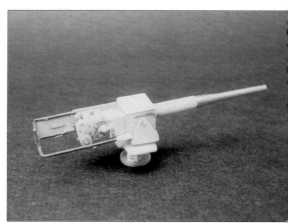

The breech in isolation before mounting. (MC)

A photo of the real Matilda tensioner. (MC)

A close-up of Mark's highly detailed idler wheel tensioner built from sheet styrene. (MC)

This view shows the level of detail on the breech of the gun. (MC)

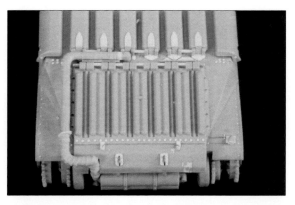

Tamiya masking tape was used to represent the asbestos on the exhaust pipe at the rear of the model. (MC)

Extra detail was added to this area too, such as the tow hooks. (MC)

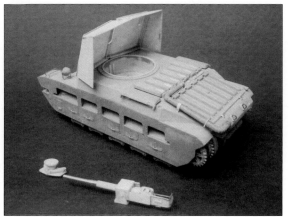

The breech, shield and main body are shown here ready for assembly. Note the hollowed-out kit sprocket wheels in the rear. (MC)

locate a suitable part from an existing kit, he opted to scratchbuild the gun completely. From his contacts in the Internet modelling community, Mark managed to locate a series of detailed drawings and measurements of the 5cm L/42 gun assembly.

Having obtained this information, the next step was to figure out how to recreate the stepped design of the barrel. The most obvious method was with a lathe, but since Mark does not own one, he used a Dremel multi-tool. This worked very well not only in producing a barrel within an acceptable margin of error, but in reducing the diameter of the Elefant barrel, which was slightly too wide.

Due to the high speed of the tool, it took four attempts at turning styrene rod before he achieved a satisfactory barrel in one-piece with a margin of error of less than 0.2mm diameter. To do this he inserted a 4mm-wide styrene rod into the Dremel and used an assortment of files and sandpaper to replicate the stepped design of the barrel. The diameter of the barrel was constantly checked during this process using a set of electronic calipers Mark had borrowed for the project.

The breech was based on the scale drawings on the L/42 and an assortment of photos taken from his references. Although you might think that the breech would take a great deal of time and effort to complete, the whole sub-project

The assembled model, in starboard view, before priming. (MC)

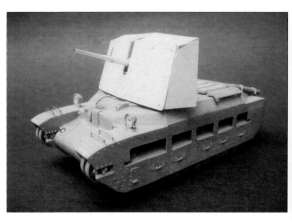

The assembled model, in port view. (MC)

The Oswald received a light coat of Tamiya Neutral Grey (XF-53) through an airbrush with a 50/50 mix of Tamiya Paint Thinner X-20A. (MC)

A first camo pattern is applied using a mix of Vallejo Neutral Grey 992 mixed with Vallejo German Grey 995 in a ratio of 4:1. A few drops of water were also added to the mix to keep the paint from drying. The paint was applied with an '00' brush. (MC)

only took about two hours, which includes the time necessary to confirm the details and determine the proper dimensions.

With the gun and breech completed, the next step was the construction of a gun mount. Since none of the photos showed the Oswald's mount, Mark based the design on a Panzerjäger I which mounted a 47mm gun (as opposed to the Oswald's 50mm gun). The mount may not be correct, but Mark took the view that it was much better (and simpler) for the Germans to use an existing design than invent a new mount.

Mark next tackled the question of where and how the vehicle's gunsight was mounted. Since there is small viewport cut into the right hand side of the gunshield, Mark's initial assumption was to place the sight in this location. However, while researching the gun, it became apparent that the viewport was on the wrong side. It is possible that the gunsight was repositioned during the conversion process. However, after looking at other photos of German SPGs, Mark decided to keep the gunsight on the left-hand side of the gun and mount a pair of scissor periscopes.

As there is no evidence of tools or tool brackets on the Oswald in the available photos, Mark elected to shave off the simplified kit details and fill the various mounting holes in the hull.

With the kit constructed, it was time for the painting process. With only a few black and white photos on hand, determining the colours and scheme

became a question of considering the location, timeframe and purpose of the vehicle. Initially, Mark thought that perhaps the Oswald sported a late-war scheme of dark yellow, red brown and green. But noting the date and location of the photos, he quickly discarded this idea in favour of a mixture of greys and black. His reasoning for the choice of colours is based on several factors. Since the Matilda was considered to be unsuitable for frontline service, it is unlikely that there would have been an official conversion program. This hypothesis is backed up by the lack of care displayed in the construction of the gun shield.

As such, it is most likely that a conversion such as the Oswald would have been a local project using local talent and resources. Given that the conversion was made in the early 1940s, during the period that German forces were preparing for the invasion of Britain (Operation Sea Lion), there would have been large stocks

A first weathering treatment of Raw Umber and Burnt Sienna oils mixed with Testors thinners was applied to the whole tank to accentuate shadows and add depth. (MC)

A second weathering treatment was undertaken comprising the same oil mix, but this time locally applied to bolts and rivets. Then, a dry-brush of Humbrol 155 Grey was applied to the whole tank to highlight the bolts and raised surface areas. (MC)

The finished Oswald placed on a scenic base: a calendar picture of a stretch of French coastline was used for the background setting. (MC)

A front view of the finished Oswald. (MC)

of naval colours available for the various vessels and barges intended to ferry the invasion force across the Channel. In addition, one of the photos of the Oswald shows the tank on such a militarised barge, and both carry identical colour schemes.

Before painting, the model was cleaned with soap and water and allowed to dry for a few hours. The kit was then primed with a light coat of Tamiya Neutral Grey XF-53 mixed with 30 per cent Tamiya Thinners X-20. This was allowed to dry and a thorough inspection of the surface revealed a few flaws, which required some sanding and filing. The kit (less the tracks) was then sprayed with a second light coat of Neutral Grey, which acts as both a primer and base coat. This was allowed to dry overnight, after which a gloss coat was applied to protect the kit from subsequent weathering.

With his reference photos to hand, Mark applied a mix of Vallejo Neutral Grey (992) mixed with 20 per cent Vallejo German Grey (995) for the first camouflage scheme. The paint was mixed with a few drops of tap water to provide ease of flow. With a '00' brush, Mark applied the light-coloured camouflage scheme and closely matched the black and white wartime photos of the Oswald. This was allowed to dry for about 30 minutes.

A second camo application was applied with a mix of Vallejo Neutral Grey (992) mixed with 80 per cent Vallejo Black Grey (950). The paint was again mixed with a few drops of water and was applied with a '00' brush. This was left to dry overnight.

Next it was time to apply the markings, which were Archer Fine Transfers Balkenkreuz. The Archer transfers had to be reduced by almost 1mm in diameter in order to fit the sides. Mark accomplished this by carefully trimming the decals with a clean blade. The modified transfers were then carefully applied using a pencil and toothpick, the latter serving to apply the decals around the various rivets on the hull. Once the

markings were in place, the model was given a light satin finish using Testors Clear from an aerosol can.

The kit was then lightly airbrushed with Humbrol thinner to break up the surface tension. An equal mix of Raw Umber and Burnt Sienna oils were mixed with 60 per cent Humbrol Thinners and lightly applied with a wide brush to the entire surface of the kit. A second wash of Raw Umber mixed with thinners was applied to all of the cracks and along seam and joints with a '00' brush. This was left to dry for one hour.

A light dry-brushing of Humbrol Matt Gull Grey 140 was done on all surfaces allowing the brush to catch all of the rivets. A dash of Humbrol Matt White was then applied to the Gull Grey and again, the surface was lightly dry-brushed to create a subtle tonal difference.

With a fine '000' brush, a mix of Burnt Sienna oils paints and Humbrol thinner (1:1 mix) was applied locally to the rivets and bolts, particularly along the side track guards. Some of the Burnt Sienna was drawn down with a dry '000' brush to denote rust runs.

The kit's vinyl tracks were primed in Tamiya Matt Black and dry-brushed with steel paint followed by various earth tones including Humbrol Matt Earth (26), Matt Khaki (77) and Matt Ochre (88). The tracks were slipped into place and attached at the rear with copper wire.

The last stage was to spray a light mist of Tamiya Buff XF-57 on the lower substructure of the Oswald, also applying a light coat to the tracks, which helped blend the lower part of the kit with the tracks.

Mark admits that the hardest part of the entire project was gathering the necessary reference material. Although he has developed a substantial reference library, a number of detail questions remain unanswered. Overall, the project presented a number of challenges, but there were few major obstacles that a little planning and work failed to overcome. It also shows that even though the basic Tamiya kit is an old one, a little creative thinking can result in a very satisfying modelling project.

Not much to do! A figure was added to the scene to bring it to life. (MC)

Museums, collections and reference

In this chapter, rather than attempt to provide a dry list of every Matilda type and variant and their museum or collection location, I thought it would be more useful to show the vehicles themselves in colour photos. There are numerous examples in museums all over the world, particularly Britain, Australia, the United States, and Canada. For those who are not able to see the 'Tilly' in the flesh, I hope that the photos in this chapter will provide you with some good reference and perhaps some modelling ideas. I have also included a quick-reference chart of the types and usage of the Matilda variants, together with a brief description.

An Infantry Tank Mark II at the US Army Ordnance Museum at Aberdeen Proving Grounds, Maryland, USA. (MC)

A superb example of an Infantry Tank Mark II in a desert three-colour Caunter scheme, located at the Musée des Blindés, Saumur, France. (EP)

Matilda types and uses

A12 Matilda Senior	Mild steel pilot model.
A12E1	Pilot model with six mud chutes in side skirts.
Black Prince	Radio-control version of the Matilda IIB.
Infanterie Panzer Mk II 748(e)	Captured Matilda used by the Germans.
Matilda I A12E2, Infantry Tank Mark II	The first production type, with AEC engines.
Matilda I [France model]	Matilda I modified in France during 1939–40 to include a tail skid and raised suspension.
Matilda IM Infantry Tank Mark IIM	Mild steel training tank.
Matilda II Infantry Tank Mark IIA	Besa machine gun replacing the Vickers.
Matilda Infantry Tank Mark IIA/M	Mild steel training tank.
Matilda IIB A12E2	
Matilda Infantry Tank Mark IIB/M	Mild steel training version of the Matilda IIB.
Matilda IICS	Fitted with 3in. howitzer.
Matilda II CDL	'Canal Defence Light', fitted with De Thoren flashing arc light.
Matilda II TLC	Fitted with carpet-laying device.
Matilda III Infantry Tank Mark IIA	Leyland diesel engines added.
Matilda IIICS	Fitted with 3in. howitzer for close-support suppressive fire.
Matilda IV Infantry Tank Mark IIA	Similar to the Mk.III but with improved Leyland engines and Clayton Dewendre air servo transmission.
Matilda IVCS	Fitted with 3in. howitzer for close-support smoke.
Matilda V Infantry Tank Mark IIA	Fitted with Westinghouse air servo, and improved gear box and gear shaft.
Matilda V CDL	'Canal Defence Light', Matilda V fitted with De Thoren flashing arc light.
Matilda [Australian]	
Matilda [Bangalore]	Matilda adapted to carry and project a length of Bangalore torpedo.
Matilda [Cromwell]	Fitted with Cromwell turret.
Matilda [Experimental Crane]	Crane device.
Matilda Hedgehog	Fitted with rear-mounted 5 spigot-type rocket-launcher.
Matilda Inglis Bridge	Light bridge on a track pushed ahead of the Matilda.
Matilda [Torpedo Mortar]	Fitted with 2in. anti-mine mortar.
Matilda [Trench Crossing Device]	Middle East experimental bridging device.
Matilda AMRA Mark IA	Mine clearing. Matilda-based mine roller device.
Matilda Baron I	Mine clearing. Flail tank version with chain and sprocket drive.
Matilda Baron II	Mine clearing. Rebuilt Baron I with shaft-drive from six-cylinder Bedford engines.
Matilda Baron III	Mine clearing. Version with lower perambulator-type flail.
Matilda Baron IIIa	Mine clearing. Mine clearing. Turretless version of the Baron III.
Matilda Carrot	Anti-mine roller device with single deflection shield.
Matilda Dozer No 1 Mark I	Australian dozer tank with Britsand box-shaped dozer blade.
Matilda Dozer No 3 Mark I	Australian dozer tank.
Matilda Dozer Mark I	Australian improvised dozer tank.
Matilda Dozer Mark 2	Australian improvised dozer tank.
Matilda Frog Mark I	Australian flamethrower version based on Matilda IV and V with flamethrower.
Matilda Murray	Australian-developed flamethrower version similar to Frog.
Matilda Heavy Carrot	600 lbs of high-explosive demolition charge.
Matilda Lobster	Mine clearing. Crab-type rotor arms with Baron-type rotor and flail.
Matilda Plough	Fitted with truncated AMRA frame, large ploughshares and truck wheels.
Matilda Scorpion Flail [Prototype]	Mine clearing. Tank with flail on lattice girder.
Matilda Scorpion I	Mine clearing. Flail tank with flail operator in armoured box beside right track.
Matilda Scorpion II	Mine clearing. Flail tank with simplified lattice girder.

ABOVE A lend-lease Matilda III CS Infantry Tank with 3in. howitzer on display at the Tank Museum of the Red Army, Kubinka, Russia. (PZ)

BELOW A British Infantry Tank Mark II 'Matilda' used in the Western Desert, now on display at the Imperial War Museum, London, UK. It is missing its exhausts. (SG)

Frontal view of an Infantry Tank Mark II at the Tank Museum, Bovington, UK. This tank was originally used as a training vehicle and was repainted in the desert Caunter scheme. (SG)

A close-up of the left hull side of the Bovington Matilda. The *Golden Miller* was the tank of Maj. Gen. Bob Foote, who commanded the 7th Royal Tank Regiment and was awarded the Victoria Cross. (LM)

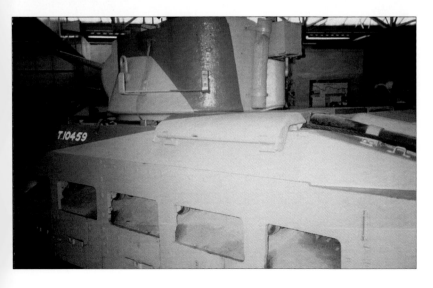

A detailed shot of the right hull side of the Bovington Matilda. (LM)

ABOVE An Australian Frog at the Melbourne Tank Museum, Narre, Victoria. (MG)

BELOW This Matilda III Infantry Tank is on display at the Victory Memorial in Moscow, Russia. It has a fake mantlet. (PZ)

ABOVE Side view of the Mk II Matilda at the Royal Museum of the Army and Military History, Brussels, Belgium. (LM)

Close up of the turret of the 'Grimsby' Mk II Matilda at the Royal Museum of the Army and Military History, Brussels, Belgium. (LM)

Detailed front view of the Matilda 'Grimsby' in Brussels. (LM)

ABOVE A superbly restored Infantry Tank Mk II Matilda housed at the New South Wales Lancers Memorial Museum, Australia. (DC/JH)

BELOW A rare and very fine example of an Australian Matilda dozer, at the Royal Australian Armoured Corps Memorial and Army Tank Museum, Puckapunyal, Australia. (BR)

ABOVE A close-up of the Puckapunyal museum's dozer showing
the attachment to the main body. (BR)

BELOW A restored Frog, in Puckapunyal, Australia. (BR)

Further reading and research

Fletcher, David *Matilda Infantry Tank 1938–1945*, New Vanguard series No. 8, Osprey Publishing Ltd. Oxford, ISBN 1 85532 457 1 (1994)

Crow, Duncan. (Ed) *British AFVs 1919–1940*, Profile Publications Ltd., ISBN 85383 001 0 (1970)

White, B.T. *British Tank Markings and Names*, Squadron/Signal Publications, ISBN 0 89747 080 X (1978)

Handel, P. *Dust, Sand and Jungle: A History of Australian Armour 1927–1948*, Royal Australian Armoured Corps Memorial and Army Tank Museum, ISBN 1 87643 975 0

Handel, P. *The Matilda Infantry Tank In Australian Service*, Military Ordnance Special Number 13, Darlington Publications, Inc. (1996)

Harns, N and Clayton, S. *British Armour in Action*, Squadron/Signal Publications (1974)

Hodges, P. and Taylor, M. *British Military Markings 1939–45*, Cannon Publications, ISBN 1 899695 00 1 (1971)

Chamberlain, P. and Ellis, C. *British and American Tanks of World War Two*, Cassel & Co, ISBN 0 304 35529 1 (1969)

Perrett, Bryan *The Matilda – Armour in Action*, Ian Allan Ltd., ISBN 0 71100 405 6

Zaloga, Steve *Blitzkrieg – Armour Camouflage and Markings 1939–1940*, Arms & Armour Press, ISBN 0 85368 334 4 (1980)

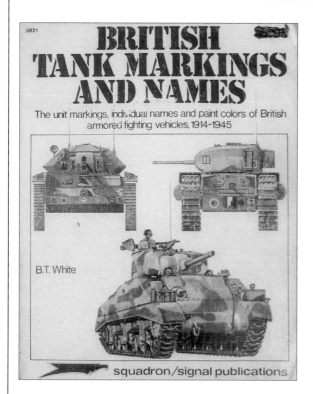

British Tank Markings and Names, by B.T. White (Squadron/Signal Publications): out of print, but can be found. (HM)

Blitzkrieg: Armour Camouflage and Markings 1939–1940, by Steve Zaloga (Arms & Armour Press, ISBN 0 85368 334 4). (HM)

The ideal home resource centre: a section of my friend Paul Fraser's personal library. (HM)

British Armour in Action, by N. Harns and S. Clayton (Squadron/Signal Publications, 1974). (HM)

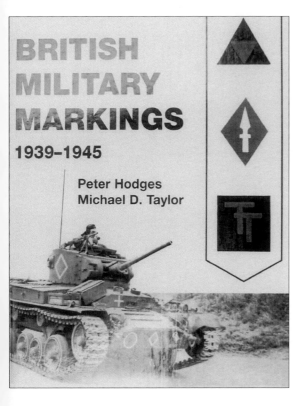

British Military Markings 1939–45, by P. Hodges and M. Taylor (Cannon Publications, ISBN 1 899695 00 1). (HM)

One of the many excellent Ground Power releases. The text is all in Japanese, but the pictures are outstanding! (HM)

Probably one of the most informative of all the books on the Matilda is New Vanguard No. 8, *Matilda Infantry Tank 1938–1945*, by David Fletcher and illustrated by Peter Sarson (Osprey Publishing Ltd.) This illustration forms the central cutaway of this book.

Websites

AFV News	www.activevr.com/afv
AFV Interiors	www.AFVInteriors.hobbyvista.com
ANZAC Steel	www.anzacsteel.hobbyvista.com
Arcane Fighting Vehicles	www.geocities.com/gpmatthews
Armour in Focus	www.armourinfocus.co.uk
Australian War Memorial	www.awm.gov.au
Battlefield in Russia	www.battlefield.ru/library/lend/matilda.html
Bovington Tank Museum	www.tankmuseum.co.uk
Canadian Tracks	www.magma.ca/~tracks
Missing-Lynx.com	www.missing-lynx.com
MVPA	www.mvpa.org/nuke/html/index.php
NSW Lancers Memorial Museum	www.lancers.org.au/museum
Perth Military Modelling	www.perthmilitarymodelling.com
RAAC	www.armytankmuseum.com.au
Royal Canadian Armd Corps Assc.	www.rcaca.org
Sentinel	www.webone.com.au/%7Emyszka
Tanks!	www.mailer.fsu.edu/~akirk/tanks

Kits and accessories available

In **1/285** scale, **GHQ Miniatures** offers two complete kits: the Matilda II (kit #04) and a GHQ Matilda Commonwealth Western Desert 1940 (kit #151).

In **1/76**, there are several options for full kits. **Cromwell Models** offers two superbly cast resin kits which come ready assembled, and offers a 1/76-scale Matilda Mk.I BEF 1940 (kit #3), as well as a Matilda A12 (kit #2). **Airfix** provides a full 1/76-scale Matilda III (kit #1318) tank in plastic with vinyl tracks, which despite its age is still quite a decent kit. **Fujimi** has a plastic offering (kit #76068) of a British Matilda III, which is slightly more detailed than the Airfix kit and poses little difficulty in assembly.

In the slightly larger **1/72** format, **ESCI** offers a 1/72-scale British Matilda in plastic. Although the kit may be difficult to find, you can purchase it through various websites.

The **1/35** modelling options for the Matilda are quite limited. **Commander's Series** offering of a 1/35-scale British Matilda Mk. 1 (Late) is a multi-media kit with 50 resin parts, 16 white-metal bits and about 50 etched-brass parts. The kit poses many challenges, as some of the parts are either inaccurate or the

ABOVE Accurate Armour's 1/35-scale multi-media A11, shown here assembled, but minus the tracks. (Derek Hansen at Accurate Armour)

ABOVE Accurate Armour's 1/35-scale A11 in finished form. (Derek Hansen at Accurate Armour)

Tamiya's 1973 plastic Matilda A12, the only one of its kind in 1/35 scale. (CM)

Airfix's 1/72-scale plastic Matilda. Easily found and very affordable. (CM)

Fujimi's 1/76-scale plastic offering. A little bit more expensive, but well-designed and highly detailed. (CM)

ESCI's 1/72-scale plastic offering of the Matilda. Often hard to find, the most effective way to get hold of it may be to check modelling websites and flea markets. (CM)

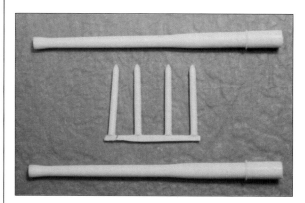

Ultracast's excellent resin 2-pdr barrels and shells. Ultracast carries several after-market products to fit the 1/35-scale Matilda. (Kevin McLaughlin at Ultracast)

Friulmodel workable metal tracks: easy to use, very authentic looking – and expensive. (CM)

Cromwell's superb 1/76-scale Combat Ready Matilda A12. (CM)

casting is flawed. It can be built up into a relatively good kit, but much work needs to be done. The kit is out of production, but can be located through various modelling websites.

The 1/35 Matilda I A11 Infantry Tank from **Accurate Armour** (kit #K67) includes 65 resin, 84 white-metal, 36 etched-brass parts, fine wire and brass rod, and a decal sheet for five different vehicles. The Accurate armour kit comes highly recommended according to several reviews in magazines and on the Internet and does not pose any difficulties.

The **Tamiya** 1/35-scale Matilda Mk.II (kit #35024) was produced in 1973 and represents one of original motorised kits. The kit has since been re-released, but never retooled or reworked. The kit is a relatively good 'skeleton' on which to start work, but some detailing is necessary. Although Tamiya's is the only complete Mk.II kit, there are several after-market products to help make this offering more accurate.

Existing **conversion** and **after-market** products to update the Tamiya kit include photoetch detail sets from **Airwaves** (#35070) and **Eduard Accessories** (#35099). **Elefant Model Accessories** offers a 45mm turned aluminium barrel (#35344) and **Jordi Rubio Accessories** offers the early British 2-pdr (#jr15) in metal. Barrels in resin form can be purchased through **MR Models** (#35148) for the Matilda II in the 40mm 2-pdr format and **Ultracast** provides an update kit that includes two Matilda 2-pdr barrels with shells (#35001).

For the **tracks**, there are two metal sets offered by **Friulmodel** – the Matilda flat-type tracks (#171) and the Matilda TD 5910 Type Tracks (#172).

MR Models also offers several interesting resin updates in 1/35 scale, including a Matilda Frog Flamethrower used by the Australians (#35146), a resin CS Tank Detail Set (#35147), and a resin turret late style with low cupola (#35149).

The Airwaves photoetch set for the Tamiya 1/35 kit. Somewhat limited in content, but ideal for those areas that require modification. (CM)

Kit list

Scale	Manufacturer	Details
1/285	GHQ Miniatures	#04 Matilda II
1/287	GHQ Miniatures	#151 Commonwealth Western Desert 1940
1/76	Cromwell Models	#003 Matilda Mk. I (BEF 1940) (resin)
1/76	Cromwell	#002 Combat Ready 002 A12 Matilda (resin)
1/76	Airfix	#1318 Matilda Mk. III Tank (plastic)
1/76	Fujimi	#76068 British Tank Matilda III (plastic)
1/72	ESCI	British Tank Matilda (plastic)
1/35	Commander Series Models	#1005 British Matilda Mk.I (Late)
1/35	Accurate Armour	#67 A11 Matilda Mk.I
1/35	Tamiya	#35024 Matilda Mk. II British Infantry Tank

Conversions and after-market kits

Scale	Manufacturer	Details
1/35	Airwaves	#35070 A12 Matilda Detail Set (photoetch)
1/35	Eduard Accessories	#35099 Matilda Mk. II Detail Set (photoetch)
1/35	Elefant Model Accessories	#35344 45mm Barrel (turned aluminium)
1/35	Friulmodel	#171 Matilda Tracks (white metal tracks)
1/35	Friulmodel	#172 Matilda TD 5910 Type Tracks (white metal tracks)
1/35	Jordi Rubio Accessories	#jr15 British 2-pdr (Early) (metal)
1/35	MR Models	#35146 Matilda II Frog Flamethrower (Australian) turret
1/35	MR Models	#35147 Matilda II CS Tank Detail Set (resin)
1/35	MR Models	#35148 Matilda II 40mm 2-pdr Conversion (resin)
1/35	MR Models	#35149 Matilda II Turret Late Style w/Low Cupola (resin)
1/35	MR Models	#35150 Matilda II CS Lathe Turned Gun Barrel/Shield
1/35	Ultracast	#35001 Mk. II Matilda 2-pdr Barrels & Shells (resin)

Index

1. Testors Medium Green FS 34102, enamel

2. Vallejo Matt Black 950 plus German Uniform Field Grey 830, acrylic

3. Polly S Pullman Green 410045, enamel

4. Humbrol Earth 26, enamel

5. Humbrol Matt Khaki Drill 72, enamel

6. Humbrol Matt Forest Green 150, enamel

7. Tamiya Buff X-53, acrylic

8. Tamiya Dark Yellow XF-60 plus Khaki XF-49, acrylic

9. Tamiya Neutral Grey XF-53, acrylic

10. Model Master RAF Interior Green 2062, enamel

11. Vallejo Neutral Grey 992 plus German Grey 995, acrylic

12. Vallejo Black 950 plus Neutral Grey 992, acrylic

13. Tamiya Khaki Drab XF-51, acrylic

14. Vallejo Dark Sand 847, acrylic

15. Humbrol Matt Desert Yellow 94, enamel

16. Polly S Grimy Black F414137, acrylic

17. Humbrol Track Colour 173, enamel

3. Polly S Pullman Green 410045, enamel

The base colour for the Frog. Research on wartime colours used by the Australians reveals that this green was darker than the British equivalent. .

2. Vallejo Matt Black 950 plus German Uniform Field Grey 830, acrylic

This is mixed in a ratio of 3:1 and was used to represent the disruptive 'Dark Bronze Green' scheme applied by field troops over 'basic factory Khaki Green'.

1. Testors Medium Green FS 34102, enamel

The base paint used for the A11 Matilda, and a close match for the wartime reference description 'basic factory Khaki Green'.

6. Humbrol Matt Forest Green 150, enamel

This was used for dry-brushing the Frog, to highlight the surface details on the tank. Adding a very small amount of Humbrol Matt White to this and repeating the dry-brushing brings out even more raised detail.

5. Humbrol Matt Khaki Drill 72, enamel

This was applied as a secondary mud layer over the Humbrol Earth.

4. Humbrol Earth 26, enamel

This is ideal for creating dirt and dried mud. Mixed with thinners, it is also good for showing fuel leakage.

9. Tamiya Neutral Grey XF-53, acrylic

A dash of white was added to make the slate blue camo colour on Sean Dunnage's Matilda. This was also the base colour on Mark Cooper's Oswald.

8. Tamiya Dark Yellow XF-60 plus Khaki XF-49, acrylic

This was mixed in a ratio of 4:1. Sean Dunnage used this mix as the base sand colour for his Matilda's Caunter scheme. Note how the yellow has a distinctive green tone.

7. Tamiya Buff X-53, acrylic

This was airbrushed on the lower hull of the Frog and the Oswald to create a dusty appearance. Apply this paint in natural light to make sure it is not overdone.

12. Vallejo Black 950 plus Neutral Grey 992, acrylic

Used by Mark Cooper for the second camo pattern on the Oswald. Mixed in a ratio of 5 parts Black to 1 part Grey. .

11. Vallejo Neutral Grey 992 plus German Grey 995, acrylic

Mixed in a ratio of 4:1. This was used by Mark Cooper for the first camo pattern on the Oswald.

10. Model Master RAF Interior Green 2062, enamel

Used by Sean Dunnage as the final camo colour for the Caunter scheme.

15. Humbrol Matt Desert Yellow 94, enamel

Humbrol provides a variant for the desert Matilda's base yellow colour, as the tones were known to differ widely. Many modellers prefer to add a little Humbrol Matt White to lighten this paint. .

14. Vallejo Neutral Grey 992 plus German Grey 995, acrylic

An ideal sand-coloured base for desert Matildas, either monotone or Caunter-schemed. The colours will vary considerably though, given factors such as exposure to the sun, and the effect of sand and wind on paint. Add green or brown to darken this tone.

13. Tamiya Khaki Drab XF-51, acrylic

Used by Steve Zaloga as the base coat for his BEF Matilda, and airbrushed on in two light coats.

17. Humbrol Track Colour 173, enamel

A good match for track colour, but not always easy to find on hobby store shelves. A close match can be achieved by mixing black and dark brown paints in equal proportion.

16. Polly S Grimy Black F414137, acrylic

An ideal colour for rubber wheels and tracks, and one of the smoothest paints to work with.